PC 24.6

Night of Anguish, Morning of Hope

Night of Anguish, Morning of Hope

Jean Mize

Jeremy Books

5624 Lincoln Drive Edina, Minnesota 55436

Jeremy Books

5624 Lincoln Drive, Edina, MN 55436

Night of Anguish, Morning of Hope
Copyright © 1979 by Jean Mize
All rights reserved. No part of this book may be reproduced in any form, except for the inclusion of brief quotations in a review, without permission in writing from the publisher.

Printed in the United States of America

Library of Congress Catalog Card Number: 79-88497
ISBN 0-89877-009-2
Sketches by Nancy Duke, aunt to Dana Mize

Dedication

In Memory of

DANA

Your sufferings have not been wasted.

Acknowledgements

I would like to say 'Thank You' to the many people who helped us:

Arkansas State Police, Federal Bureau of Investigation, Vilonia Law Enforcement Officials, Joe Martin and his Deputies, Charles Castleberry and his Deputies, Citizen Band Radio Clubs, Major W.A. Tudor, John Kelly, Lt. Ken McFerran, Dr. Rodney Carlton, Gov. David Pryor, Gov. Brendon Byrne, Lt. Richard Mason, Jim Elliott, Paul Maxwell, Allen Tuff, Ellis Joe Ogden, Dr. Rosendale, Sgt. Bill Reed, Alex Street and his staff, Judge Roberts, Jury, Yell County Officials, Dr. Revitch and his wife, Richard Hendrickson, Dr. Bob Benafield, Dr. Bob Banister, Delbert Massey, Freddie Weaver, Roland Turner, Dr. Sam Daniel, Mrs. Mary Wells, William Probasco, Randy Shannon, Ravel Loyd, Mr. & Mrs. Basil Butler, John Hicks, Donna Ridenoure, National Guard, Air Force, Margaret Turner, Donna Taylor, those who donated to the reward fund, Log Cabin Democrat, Channels 4, 7, & 11 TV Stations, friends and neighbors, and most of all, my family.

"My peace I give unto you: not as the world giveth, give I unto you. Let not your heart be troubled, neither let it be afraid."
                    John 14:27

The One Who Was, Is

by Martha Mize, grandmother to Dana Mize

The warm touches of friends add gladness to a still aching heart
But my searching glance cannot see a glint of light on flowing strands of gold from the head of the child who was
Her absence is especially felt because the family circle was complete and now is not
My mind picks up memories:
   A yellow card with a kitten in one corner, and tiny red letters that spell "I love you, Mom"
   A small hand on my arm and a whisper when Mother isn't looking—"Another cracker, please, just one more"
   A box of treasures laid out in a row
   A precious moment of sharing
   A dress wrinkled from a long ride, because "I wanted you to see it"
   Words flowing over each other in excitement after a special time
   Arms clasped around my middle, while joy spills from the depth of her sparkling blue eyes
   A new kitten, a new puppy—she loved them all
   A rock (her favorite) nestled in tissue and gift-wrapped for me
She isn't with me anymore
I can't see clearly; the tears I've been fighting come, anyway
The memories are too few
But why am I sad?
After a small number of tomorrows, this child who still lives and I will have part in an eternity of sharing
and go hand-in-hand looking for more treasures

Introduction

April 16, 1976
"The body of twelve-year-old Dana Diane Mize, daughter of Mr. and Mrs. Rodney Mize of Vilonia, was recovered this morning in a pond near Conway. She was abducted near her home Tuesday evening, taken to an isolated area, beaten, raped, strangled, and thrown into the pond to drown."

Although it has been more than a year since it happened, it seems only yesterday that our little girl was murdered. There have been many times since when the case has been mentioned in the paper or on television; yet it still shocks me to hear the actual words. I continue to find myself laying the table for six or saying I have four children . . . but I am slowly adjusting to her absence.

God has revealed so much about Himself this year as He has comforted us and helped us through this traumatic time. I want to share some of these special things with you, not to show you how great or strong we are, but to show you how great God is, and how He will lift us above the worst of situations. I want to tell you the great truth we have learned through the experience that led to the loss of our beloved Dana—that God will provide the sustaining power that will see you triumphant through any problem.

God is truly sufficient! Before Dana's death, I would be worried if any of my children were even ill. The peace and calm we were given to face her death were supernatural, and not normal human reactions to pain and worry.

I want to tell you how God revealed the truth concerning His will in our lives. "His ways are not our ways" became a reality as we desired a way *out* of our circumstances, but He showed us the path *through* them. We can know God's will only by knowing Him; as we sought Him, He revealed a portion of that will to us.

I read somewhere that our lives are like a large tapestry. God is doing the weaving and from His side it is beautiful, but underneath where we see, there are only knots and ravels. Though God has not allowed us to view the whole piece, I thank Him that He has seen fit to show us a glimpse of the pattern. I thank Him that when things seemed utter chaos to me, He could weave order, and when they were totally ugly, He could bring beauty.

—Jean Mize

A Note from the Publisher

When we read Jean Mize's account of her daughter's tragic murder, we were moved by the unquestioning way she accepted what the Lord revealed to her through Scripture. Yet, we were a bit uncomfortable with the apparent absence of normal grief on her part. Was it merely the balm of time, the fact that she was looking back, that subdued her grief? In Mrs. Mize's words:

"I have prayed and tried to write differently, but that would be unfaithful to the revealed word of God, and nothing, not even publishing this book, is that important to me.

"I've based my life on a God who parted the Red Sea, turned water into wine, and caught up one of His own in a fiery chariot. My God has the power of the universe at His fingers, and He offers it to me, if I come to Him with hands that have been cleansed in His blood. Because of this, our family has lived with miracles. It's a normal part of our lives.

"Outside of our family, though, we usually don't talk of these miracles. My husband Rod read some of this manuscript, and commented 'Honey, I've lived with you for 25 years, and I know this is all true, but it's still hard to believe the way God answers your prayers.'

"We've been amazed at the continual questioning we receive concerning our accepting attitudes and actions following Dana's death. We are not unique in these. There have been so many others who have gone through similar or worse experiences, and demonstrated God's strength.

"None of us ever knows what we can do before a need arises. Monday of that fateful week, if someone had asked Rod and me 'How would you act if your daughter was kidnapped and murdered?' Rod would have said 'I'd catch the guy, tear his head off, and feed it to him.' I would have said 'I'd lose my mind.' This is the way we felt, but that is the beautiful thing about a relationship with the Lord—we don't have to rely on feelings. We can rely on Him. He is everything we need in every circumstance. Today, if something happened to one of our other children, I can't guarantee how we would act, but we do know from experience that God gives us the power to act as He would have us act. Whether we use that power or not is up to us.

"It seems there are times when there is a need for me to shed tears and there are other times when that need is not there. It does not matter to me which the Lord wants, just as long as He gives me the strength to do His will.

"His peace, and His strength, really is not at all like anything the world can give—or even comprehend. We don't understand it, but we praise Him for His comfort."

A Special Message from the Author

I pray this book will not be used by you, the reader, as a guideline of how you should act in the time of grief. No one except you and God can decide what your actions should be. I do want you to see, however, that there may be times in your life when things are too much for you to bear alone and Christ will give you the strength to bear it if you seek His face.

Some have said that God allowed this to happen to us because we were so strong; but the opposite is true. I Cor. 1:27-29 says, "God hath chosen the foolish things of the world to confound the wise; and God hath chosen the weak things of the world to confound the things which are mighty; and base things of the world, and things which are despised, hath God chosen, yea, and things which are not, to bring to nought things that are: That no flesh should glory in His presence."

We were chosen so that when God gave us such peace everyone would know that it could come only from Him.

Learning who the Lord is, what things He has promised to do, what He expects of us, and how much He loves us is a slow process.

I thank God I had known Him as a personal friend for over 30 years when Dana was killed. Because of this I knew many facets of His personality that I could depend on. Had I not had them I could never have placed Dana confidently in His hands and trusted His will for us all.

Because of thousands of miraculous answers we've had through the years, we knew God could do anything. We also knew He loves us so much that whatever He chooses will be for our best.

Sometimes our best was for Him to say "No." Once my sister was ill and feared for her life. She called and asked me to ask the Lord whether she was dying. I prayed and went to my Scripture for the day. In Ezekiel 20:3, I found, "Thus saith the Lord God; are ye come to inquire of me? As I live, saith the Lord God, I will not be enquired of by you." I called her back and told her the Lord had said for me to mind my own business.

It was the lifetime habit of going to the Lord with our problems that helped us when we needed Him most. It was His faithfulness in the past that gave us the confidence that He could take care of us now and in the future.

ONE
Wait

"Rest in the Lord, and wait patiently for him, fret not thyself because of him who prospereth in his way, because of the man who bringeth wicked devices to pass."
Psalm 37:7

On Tuesday, April 13, Rod and I had made plans to meet with our tax advisor. Lance, our sixteen-year-old son, came home early from school so he could work at our service station which provides the living for the family. Dana, our twelve-year-old daughter, planned to help out until Bill, our seventeen-year-old, came home from a track meet. After work, they were going to eat at the local dairy bar.

Dana came racing into the house as usual, dropped her purse and jacket onto the sofa, and announced, "I'm ready to go to work." She enjoyed working in the service station, for her earnings were a coke and a candy bar.

Rod said, "I'll take you to work and then come back and pick Mom up."

"Okay. See you later, Mom," and with a lift of the hand she was away. Her blonde, naturally curly hair bounced up and down in the long ponytail that hung down her back as she skipped to the car. Her turquoise pantsuit was a little short on her but she couldn't have cared less, for she was happy with her world.

The business with the income tax took longer than we had expected. It was half past six before we arrived home.

Renee, our oldest daughter, had returned from her work as secretary of our church and was reading.

"Where is everyone?" I asked.

"The note says they are at the Dairy Queen eating," she replied.

Rod was in the race for Faulkner County Judge, and we were both tired from the campaigning, so he switched on the television and I began work on some of the campaign posters.

Bill and Lance came home five or ten minutes before seven. They came through the door discussing the great shots they had in their pool game. I waited for Dana to come in and when she didn't, I asked, "Where's Dana?"

"Isn't she with you?" the boys asked in unison.

"No, she's supposed to be with you."

"When we came home after closing the station, she wasn't here, so we thought you came back early and took her with you," Bill explained.

"Renee, did you see a note from her?"

"The only one I saw was from the boys," she said. "I thought she was with them."

We started searching for a note, for we are a family of note writers. When it became obvious there was none, we sent the boys to discreetly ask our neighbors with children her age if they had seen her in the afternoon. This took only a few minutes. No one had seen her.

Rod went to the fire station and school, where there were community meetings, to see if anyone had seen her or knew where she could be. Bill and Lance started going to every house.

I sat down and picked up the poster again. "Oh, Lord," I breathed, "I must keep calm. There is no reason for me to feel this upset. If I act normally, everything will be all right. I know few of the things we worry about actually happen, so let me be calm, and, please, God, let us find her soon."

When friends and neighbors began to drop in to offer help, I gave up my pretended industry and began the long process of answering questions. The phone started ringing.

A family called. "Suzy saw Dana with Sharon and her family going to Conway."

"Are you sure? She has never gone anywhere like that without permission before."

"Suzy says she is sure."

I could not believe she had done such a thing, but she was not home, so I started making calls. When we reached Sharon's family, we learned they had not even left home and had not seen Dana since school. This was only one of many false leads we were to receive in the next hours.

Rod came back with more people who were concerned and wanted to help. As they were discussing the best way to proceed, the boys came running in to say, "Miss Loyd saw Dana walking home, and as she reached the Shannon house, a silver-grey car pulled up, blocking her way. The driver leaned over and said something to her and she pointed to the house. He then leaned over further and opened the door. After a minute, she got in, and he drove off real fast."

Remembering the times I had talked with her about this kind of thing, I said, "She would never get into a car with anyone, not even a friend, without permission. I cannot believe this." Nevertheless, I felt chilled.

Someone said, "He could have told her you were sick and he would take her to you."

"She is familiar with that routine. Anyway, she is extra smart and would ask why the boys weren't coming also. I still don't believe it."

"He could have had a gun," someone added.

Then I knew! He did have a gun, and she would have gotten into the car. Because the children sometimes worked at the service station, we had told them to never argue with anyone with a gun. "Your life is more important," we had said over and over. Of course, we were thinking of the station being robbed, not of something like this. Yes, she would have obeyed us, so she would have gone.

I felt as though someone had hit me in the pit of my stomach. I knew this was not a kidnapping for ransom, for our financial position was open for all to see and it was not in a bracket that would justify the risk. The alternative was horrible, but in my heart, I knew this was abduction, the vilest of crimes.

In anguish I cried, "Oh, God, how could you? You've let me down. You've always let me know beforehand so I could be prepared, but You did not this time." For years, I had claimed the promise of John 14:29:

"And now I have told you before it come to pass, that, when it come to pass, ye might believe."

Even as these angry, rebellious, thoughts were forming, God pictured in my mind an incident that had happened two weeks earlier. On my way home from a busy day campaigning, I was mentally listing the things I needed to do. Just as I passed the Crestlawn Cemetery, the thought surfaced that we should transfer our family plots from Fayetteville to Conway. I said to myself, "What a stupid thought when I have so many urgent things to do!" Had I taken the time, I would have remembered that every thought is from either God or Satan. Satan would not benefit from my compliance to this suggestion so it must be of God. I was just too busy! Or maybe, God, in His grace, knew I could not accept the full knowledge of what was to be and let me see only enough that I would know He had been faithful.

I do not know who telephoned the sheriff. I do not remember the organization of the search parties. My stunned mind was desperately trying to adjust to the horror of the situation.

The boys joined search teams and Rod helped disperse the teams.

Renee and I went to the girls' bedroom to pray. I knew we could not handle this without God's help. We knelt by the bed and began to discuss how we should pray. I was never more aware of how important it is to use the right words so we would not ask amiss. We started by verbally listing our needs. I could name the things that pertained to us, but I could not bring myself to voice Dana's needs because I was not sure Renee really understood the situation or could stand the shock when she did. When I hesitated, she said, "Let's pray especially for Dana. She is in a place where only God can help."

"Thank you, God," I breathed, "she understands

and accepts."

We finished our list and then went to prayer. I have experienced the feeling of being before God's throne in intercession before, but never as much as at this time.

"Oh, Lord, God, every day I give You that day and everything either comes directly from You or from Satan and passes through You to reach us. This day is no different, even though it seems to be, so I know You allowed this. I know You have not lost your grip on our world. I know You still have Your hand over us. You are a God of order so You have a purpose and though I can't see how any purpose or any good could come from this, O God, I know You can. Please bring good out of it. Don't let her suffering be wasted. You've promised You will never allow more to come to us than we can bear. I can't see how any of us can bear this, but I claim this promise, knowing You have already put the power in us to meet our needs. Lord God, I don't know how to voice Dana's needs, but what I don't say, Holy Spirit, You say for me. Make Yourself known to her in a real way; let Your angels be made visible to her as they bring Your comfort. In her innocence, she cannot understand this act, so do not let her experience what is happening to her body. Lord, only let her hear Your voice, only let her feel Your touch, only let her see You. Lord, if she is alive, but hurt, please don't let her be lying somewhere out in the weather. Let her be covered, for if she is needing help she would never seek it if she is uncovered. You are in her, so You share her pain. Thank You for that truth, Lord. Others are hurting because they are sharing our pain. Show us how to comfort them.

Give us such a peace that everyone will know it could come only from You. All the things I have asked are Your promises and I claim them right now, in Jesus' precious name, Amen."

As we stood, I had a feeling of peace that is beyond my ability to describe. I don't know if it was the assurance that God would honor His promises, the confidence that when we are submissive to His plan He takes control, or whatever, but I was at peace. Nothing had changed, but deep down inside of me I felt He had already solved everything so I could rest.

We decided it would be best for Renee to pray with Bill and Lance and I would pray with Rod. This sounds simple, but with the number of people there, each wanting to speak to some member of the family, it was difficult to find the time and the place.

I called Rod into our bedroom, and as he held me in his arms, I voiced our short prayer, "Holy Lord, You know our hearts, our needs and our wants. We submit them all to You, asking You to make them into what You want them to be. Live out Your purpose in us, in Jesus' name, Amen."

Renee prayed with Lance but God protected him so he could not believe the reality of what had happened. He went on the search teams because it was expected of him; also going was easier than listening to the talking and crying that went on at the house as new people came.

Bill and Renee discussed the probability of never seeing Dana again alive, and he accepted this as true but was very angry at the person who would do such a thing. He went out fully determined her body would be recovered.

I was concerned about both sons, knowing they had a natural protective instinct, an instinct that could be encouraged by others to the point they might do something foolish. This anxiety became almost unbearable when I learned that Bill had a gun with him. Another concern was the effect on them if they were present when her body was found. I took these problems to the Lord. "O Lord, they are your children, too. I don't know Your plan for their lives, but if it could be Your will, protect them from harm, and keep them from hurting anyone else. Lord, I don't think they could live with the shock of seeing Dana's body found, so please guide them for me. Please direct me that I might deal with these problems in the way You would have me. In Jesus' name I pray, Amen."

Even though I knew our children were in God's hands and cared for by friends, it was not enough sometimes. When they were gone for awhile, the desire to see and touch them would be so great I wanted to scream. Would God ask me to give up more than one? Just as I felt I could bear the strain no longer, they would come in. God knew my needs. As soon as I touched them my fears for them subsided. I had to commit this fear to God several times.

Friends and neighbors came to stand vigil with us that long Tuesday night. One said, "I just don't know that I would have the strength if something like that happened to my family."

"Yes, you would," I replied. "For you know it is not our strength, but God's. He promised He would never allow more than we could bear, so He will see us through this." Then as a wave of longing for Dana passed over me, I clutched her hand and pleaded, "Please keep reminding me when I forget."

That night was a kaleidoscope of activity.

Some of the people were so upset they were ready to lynch anyone they could find. A young man was taken into custody because his car was the same color as reported for the abduction car. We heard, "Where's the rope?" "Let's tie him to the nearest tree," and "He doesn't deserve a chance for a trial, for what chance did he give her?"

Realizing the danger of Satan winning a victory if the wrong person was hurt, I prayed, "O God, don't let anything happen that would limit Your purpose. These people are hurting for us, but control their actions so that everything will be done in Your will. And, please, God, this community has sheltered us for nine years, so don't let this person who has taken Dana come from here to bring shame on them. They are hurt enough because it has happened here. These blessings I ask knowing You will honor them in Jesus' name, Amen."

There was a feeling of helplessness in everyone, for there were no clues from the time Dana was seen getting into the car. She and her abductor had just disappeared!

A man I did not know came up to comfort me and said, "Don't worry, she won't suffer long. They usually beat them senseless first, then rape them, so it's probably already over for her." I thought I would suffocate! As the world began to spin around me, God reminded me He was in control and I should act like it. I willed my mind to hold fast on God, and as my eyes focused on the man, I calmly shook his hand and said, "Thank you for your comfort." He walked away with a light step, feeling he had been of help, and I was more aware of God's holding and comforting me. "Thank You, God," I prayed in my heart.

Some dear friends were with us and always met our needs, whether it was ice chips or a sweater, without our even asking. Food and drink appeared at my elbow and, when I couldn't eat it, was whisked away by seemingly invisible hands. I don't know all that was done for us or by whom, but I still praise God for friends who will meet your every need in the time of trouble.

Since everyone who came wanted to know all the details, there was an endless repetition of the circumstances. To verbalize the words made them worse and sometimes it seemed more than I could bear. Silently I cried to God, "O God, I need Your comfort and strength for I can't bear to think about what she is enduring." I remembered the principle Jesus taught in Luke 6:38:

> "Give and it shall be given unto you, good measure, pressed down, and shaken together, and running over, shall men give into your bosom. For with the same measure that ye mete withal it shall be measured to you again."

So, with need of comfort, I turned to comfort others, and God met my need.

Endless times we were asked why the abduction was not reported earlier by the eyewitness. I would try to explain what prevented that, but all the time I was asking myself, "Why, dear God? Why the delay? Why the indifference?" I realized that my heart was full of anger at this neighbor for her hesitation. Knowing anger is not of God, I went to Him with a repentant heart. "O God, I confess the sin of anger against Miss Loyd. In my mind, I know You could have caused her to report the abduction earlier, if this had been Your will, so this is in Your time schedule. Forgive me for my ugly thoughts and fill me with such a love for her I'll not only forgive her but stand by her when she is criticized by others. Thank You for Your love and forgiveness, in Jesus' name, Amen."

As time slowly passed, I was not aware of it, but of the toll of continued strain. Because of this weakness I was open for Satan's attack.

A visiting teenager, lost and under the influence of Satan, took delight in following me around to say things that would shock me. A search team was reported coming in, and I went to the front porch to be one of the first to hear the report. She followed me out and sadistically said, "I bet he cut her up in little pieces and stuffed her in a well." The next thing I knew my hand was raised to strike her. That was my cue! I could go no further! As I went into the house, a dear friend and my sister, seeing my agitation, suggested I go somewhere alone and have a quiet time. I had been so involved in our problem that I had not had mine. I picked up my Bible and went into our backyard, under a tree, where the remnants of Dana's tree swing hung in mute testimony of her existence.

Even as I sat down by my child's swing, the cold, clammy feeling left and a warm calm took over. God was meeting my needs, even to the point of helping me come to Him. With deep sobs I poured out my pain to God. As I have done many times before and since, I told Him every feeling I had. "O God, I come with a broken heart. I am completely undone! I can take no more nor go any farther. How I hate this child of Satan You've allowed to torment me! I hate the criminal who could take a sweet, innocent child like Dana into such horror! Lord, I know you never said it, but I always felt you would never allow a child of Yours to be treated this way. Since You've allowed this to happen to her, will You also allow something to happen to the others? O God, I don't know what I'm saying.

"Please forgive me for my rebellious attitude. Give me a love for these as You loved those who persecuted You. I know You never promised we would be untouched by evil; forgive me for my childish attitude. I know I'm supposed to have matured enough so You would not have to feed me milk again, but, Lord, I don't feel mature right now, so feed me milk. Be gentle with me. If I only knew about Dana, I feel I could take anything else. O God, is she with You or hurt somewhere? Is she cold and wet? Lord, God, You've always directed me and told me what I needed to know. I come now as a child. As you have directed me before in your word, again direct me. You know I am at the end of my resources. Help me!"

Years ago, as I was searching for a way to know God's will for my life, I found I could pray, open my Bible, and the answer or direction I needed would be there. For some time as I grew in my Christian faith, that was how He had directed me. Then there came a time there was no answer, only confusion. Brokenheartedly, I felt God had deserted me. I started back with the basics; confessing my sins, I again went to His word and found Hebrews 5:12-14:

"For when for the time ye ought to be teachers, ye

have need that one teach you again which be the first principles of the oracles of God; And are become such as have need of milk, and not of strong meat. For everyone that useth milk is unskillful in the Word of righteousness: for he is a babe. But strong meat belongeth to them that are of full age, even those who by reason of use have their senses exercised to discern both good and evil."

I realized He did not want me to have such drastic directions, but He expected me to walk in the knowledge He had already given me. From that day I began a systematic reading of the Bible. I read through the whole Bible, then started over again. God always gave me in His Word the answers I needed for that time. Sometimes it was a principle, a word of encouragement, or an admonition, but He always revealed Himself to me where my need was. Then there was another transformation when this was also stopped and I found I was to walk by faith knowing God would stop me or redirect my step when I strayed.

At this point in my life, though, I needed the milk instead of the meat. I opened my Bible to the Scripture for the day. Because of the circumstance, I had forgotten where I was to read until that moment. As I looked at Revelation 21, I knew that in the fourth verse God was giving me my answer:

"God shall wipe away all tears from their eyes; and there shall be no more death, neither sorrow, nor crying, neither shall there be any more pain, for the former things are passed away."

I went back to God and cried, "O God, do You mean

she's with You?" I wondered if my subconscious could have remembered this passage and led me to voice my question about Dana. I did not want a false answer, so I went to God again. "As a baby You would deal with, give me a Scripture to confirm Your message, if that's what You mean."

This time, with eyes closed, I let the Bible open where it would. When I opened my eyes, the verse I first saw was Jeremiah 22:10.

"Weep ye not for the dead neither bemoan him."

I sobbed, "Lord, God, I thank You and praise Your name for taking her unto Yourself!"

In my mind's eye, I saw her being comforted by Jesus Himself. Then, as I realized the permanent separation, I said, "O Precious Lord, I don't question Your calling her unto Yourself, but You are a God of order and purpose. Help me understand Your purpose in this so I can bear the separation."

With closed eyes, I again opened my Bible as God guided my fumbling hands — and there it was, His message, clearly and unmistakably in Isaiah 55:8.

"For my thoughts are not your thoughts neither are your ways my ways, saith the Lord."

I cried, "No, Lord, no matter what good could come of it, I could never have willingly given her up. I'm not like You, in that love You bore us, that I could freely give her."

For the first time, I could understand a little about God's pain in giving up Jesus, His Son.

"Thank You for being willing to give Your Son so

that through His death and resurrection Dana is now with You, and some day I'll see her again."

Then I continued to read,

"For as the heavens are higher than the earth, so are my ways higher than your ways, and my thoughts than your thoughts."

Sobbing, I said, "Yes, Lord, You see the overall plan where I can only see the part where my pain is."

The scripture goes on,

"For as the rain cometh down and the snow from heaven, and returneth not thither, but watereth the earth and maketh it bring forth the bud, that it may give seed to the sower and bread to the eater: so shall my Word be that goeth forth out of my mouth; it shall not return unto me void, but it shall accomplish that which I please and it shall prosper in the thing whereto I sent it."

"O God, I think I understand. Through her death some will come to life and even though I don't understand it all, I have Your promise You will accomplish Your will in this. Thank You."

I recalled with clarity when Dana was converted. She was five years old and the children and I were having our family time. We discussed how Jesus died because of His love for us. She was quiet during our prayer time but later asked me to talk with her. We sat on the side of her bed and talked. She was heartbroken because of the burden her sins were on Jesus, and even more so to know He had already forgiven her, if she prayed the prayer of repentance. We knelt there beside her bed and

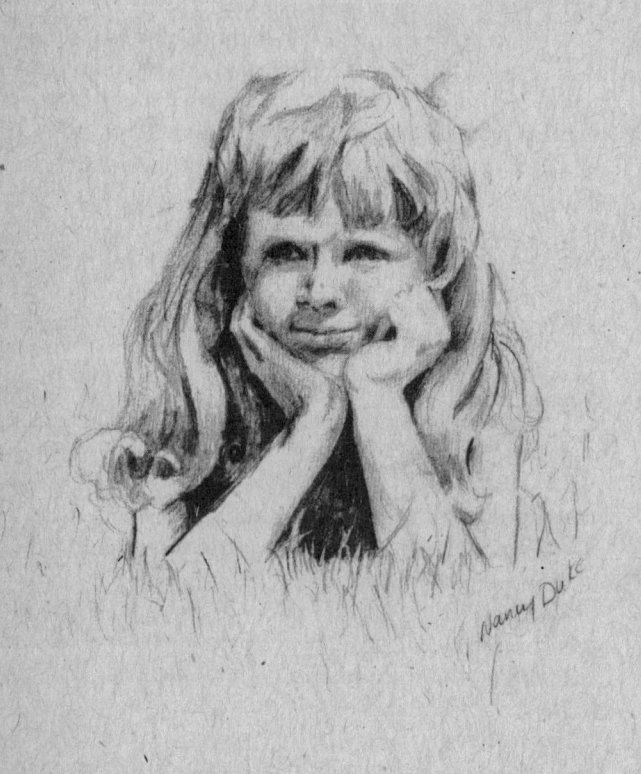

in her own words she told Jesus of her love for Him and asked Him to come live in her heart. When she stood, there was a smile on her face and she threw her arms around my neck and said, "Now I can go to Heaven, too!" How precious is that memory!

She had not been that excited about baptism, though. She said, "If I have to be baptized, I don't want to join the church." Knowing God would give her the desire for this in His time, we committed this to Him. About a month later, during the invitation, her little hand crept into mine. I opened my eyes, looking down at her. Neither of us spoke, but we walked down the aisle for her to be obedient in the first thing God called her to do. This was really a hard decision for her since she had a horror of water. The people in the church understood this, and authorized my dad to baptize her.

Later, at the age of nine or ten, she heard a sermon and became concerned about whether she had really said the right words to become a Christian. Following a lengthy discussion, I suggested we get on our knees and do it over again for her assurance. Suddenly, from the grin on her face, I knew she was sure, and she said, "I don't need to, I know He lives in me!"

Knowing doubt to be a real problem, I started her on daily Bible reading and a prayer time of her own. This was a way God could reaffirm His relationship with her. She never doubted again.

I remembered the story I had told in Children's Church entitled "Trees." There were three trees and each had a plan for its life. One wanted to be a cradle but was made into a manger. The shame the little tree felt turned into joy as the Son of God was laid there. The second wanted to be a great sailing vessel but was made into a plain fisherman's boat. His hurt was changed into joy though, when Jesus used him to teach from. The third did not want to be cut down at all but to forever point people to God, so when he was made into a cross, he was upset. Then he realized he would always be a reminder of the love God had for everyone. Not one of these trees was granted the exact wish he desired. Still each was used by God in a more glorious way than it could have dreamed. After each triumph, the story would say, "And the trees in the forest clapped their hands in joy at the beautiful plan God worked."

This truly was not what we had planned for Dana's life but I felt the joy of anticipating God's beautiful plan knowing that He brings good out of something bad. "Thank You, God, for bringing this to my mind."

He was going to bring good from evil, get glory unto Himself, and it would have eternal value. "O God, I thank You for allowing us to be the ones You would use to bring Yourself glory, and I know because Dana belonged to You, she did not experience death but the joy of going to be with You. Anything You start You will finish, so I pray You will lead us in each action that it might be what You would have it be. Please prepare the family now as I tell them about Dana. In Jesus' Holy Name, Amen."

There is a little chorus that says, "I was walking, and leaping and praising God. Walking and leaping and praising God. In the name of Jesus Christ of Nazareth, rise up and walk."

That is what I felt as I left my quiet time; but, knowing people, I had to make myself be calm. Even then there was such a change in me that several noticed, and one said, "You look like a different person." I was.

I had gone out in agitation, anger, hurt, and bewilderment, and I came back in joy, peace, and contentment. I wondered what they would do if I did walk, and leap, and praise God. It didn't take long to find out.

When one friend saw me now, he thought I was in shock. Sitting me down, he began to lecture me. "You have to settle down and rest. This isn't natural to act as you are. I know what you are feeling, and bottling it up inside you will cause you to lose your mind. Let loose! What you really need is some medication, not something strong, but enough to make you rest, for you can't continue as you are."

I interrupted, "Don't you see, I don't need anything now? I've had my quiet time and given all my problems to God. That's the reason I'm the way I am."

"You really don't understand what is happening. That's why you're like this. You are refusing to accept reality. That's why you need rest now because when it really hits you, you'll need your strength. One of your doctor friends would be glad to give you something."

"No," I said. "I really do understand and I could not be like this of my own power. Only God could let me have this peace! Don't you worry about me but take care of yourself."

It was beautiful how God worked out time schedules so I could be with one family member at a time. Renee and I went for a drive and I shared what God had given me. "I have known from the beginning she would be killed," she said. "Now I just want her body found."

The weather forecast was for rain Tuesday but it had not rained. Since we thought rain might hinder the search for her body, we listed this with our other prayer requests. I parked the car alongside the road and we prayed." "Dear Lord, thank You for the way You love us and comfort us. Thank You Dana is with You and beyond any pain or evil this world holds. We realize people do not understand us and will understand even less when it is known Dana is dead. This is not our problem but Yours. You put the understanding in their hearts. Lord, if it be Your will, let her body be found, and Lord, I know Your time schedule is not mine, so please help me accept Yours. Lord, I know You created the world and control it. You also know rain is in the forecast, but please hold it back until her body is found. I know that in Your time she will be found and not even rain can stop that, but for our peace of mind, I ask it. Thank You Precious Lord, in Jesus' name. Amen."

Later while Rod and I went for a drive, I shared with him the Scripture God had given me. We had a short prayer of commitment and, though we shed tears, it was as much out of thanksgiving that she was now safe as out of sorrow for her permanent absence from the family.

God had already prepared my sons' hearts for His message. Lance accepted Dana's death as a shadowy reality. Bill had already accepted her death. The Scripture only confirmed his belief. His anger seemed gone, but the determination to find her body was reinforced.

The FBI had been called in as is usual in cases of this type. When they first came, although they were concerned, I knew from the questions they asked that they thought Dana had run away. After one of these sessions, Rod held me as I cried, "How can they ask those questions? Don't they think we know our own child? She would never do such a thing! I just want to shake them! They're wasting all this time when they should be out looking for her."

Rod reassured me, "Honey, this happens every day. A girl disappears and her parents are sure she would not run away but later they find out it's true. Just don't say anything and give them time. They'll find out Dana wasn't like that."

Once they asked permission to look at the contents of Dana's purse, thinking it might give them some clue. As I agreed, I thought, "They still think she's a runaway or they would not expect a clue from her purse." We went into the girls' room and I emptied her purse, silently praying, "O God, this is Dana's testimony to these men, so I ask, please, don't let there be anything that would not bring glory to Yourself." I picked up one item at a time, and my heart almost burst with love and gratitude to God! There was a hairbrush with some of her lovely blonde hair, a lip gloss (no twelve-year-old would be without), a small white New Testament, a coin purse with a small amount of change, a few pencils and a pen, a test paper with a 100% grade, an envelope with a clipping of her Cousin Susan's hair, and a small notebook. I glanced idly through the notebook and found a memo that she was memorizing the 103rd Psalm. I made a mental note to read it later in her Living Bible. With a carefree heart, I talked with them about Dana. I felt they were impressed with the articles and I breathed, "I praise You, Lord, for this testimony. Please reveal to me things in my possession that would not bring glory to You."

Although I was wary at first, I grew to love and respect these men of the law who are so harassed.

Instead of being the hardhearted men I expected, they were the most gentle — yet involved — men I have ever met. I praise God for them and the many other officials who helped us. I'm sure sometimes they had a hard time understanding us, but they always tried to see our viewpoint. They were compassionate, as if our missing child were their own.

Once they came to get a list of every male we knew so they could start eliminating people who could not have taken Dana. Since we had no proof the abductor had a gun or that she would not get into a car of a friend, they were working on the assumption she had known him. The only place we could have a minute of privacy was in our bedroom, so this is where we met. There were no chairs, so we had to sit either on the king-size bed or on the floor. One of the officers, Nancy, Renee, and I chose the four corners of the bed. All of the family was taking turns naming people we knew. One person was named, and we were discussing his recent strange behavior. When the officer on the bed teasingly cautioned us to look at facts, not at our likes and dislikes, my brother Herman Hurd, with his dry humor said, "You better watch out or we'll report the fact that you were on the bed with three women." Suddenly the situation seemed so ludicrous all I could do was laugh. The others were infected and like idiots we laughed until I was embarrassed. The laughter almost turned to tears as I apologized, "I guess it is better to laugh than to cry." These men, who had seen situations like this many times before, understood we needed this near-hysterical release of tension and laughed with us.

On another occasion two of the FBI men wanted to see us in private. "What is this we hear about your little girl being an epileptic?"

As remembrance came, my heart nearly hammered out of my body. I had asked God not to let Dana be aware of what happened to her body but I had no idea until now how it was to be accomplished. I explained to them, "Dana had brain damage at birth and when she was six years old she began having blackouts. The doctors discovered she was an epileptic and prescribed medication. She could not become too tired, lose much sleep, or get too excited or she would black out, so we had to keep a watch on her. She has since outgrown the need for medication but still required the rest." They thanked me and reassured me she would be found and would be all right. I said, "God has given me Scripture showing she is already dead and in heaven with Him."

They were shocked, "Don't give up hope. Have faith and never give up."

I explained, "It is such a relief to know she is beyond being hurt anymore, especially when you consider the alternatives. I'm so sure of God's Word that if she is found alive, I will consider God has raised her as He did Jairus' daughter and given her back to us as a gift. I have not been able to pray for this, for I've felt this was not God's will."

Whatever they thought about our outlook on death, they worked relentlessly beyond their duty.

Different people came to comfort us, and the most amazing things happened. It was as though a sign was around their necks saying what their problem was, and after a few minutes we would be discussing it. I'm shocked now at some of the things I said, for I would scold, exhort, and instruct, knowing God was directing me in a marvelous way.

On several occasions, precious Christian women had a sign that said "lack of submission." One time a discussion started with the wife listing her husband's lack of attention, lack of church attendance, and lack of family participation. Then she said, "Oh, how I wish my husband could be like your husband. He shows how much he cares by being so attentive to you, never misses a Sunday at church, and all of you do things together."

That was my cue! "Until three or four years ago, my husband was like yours. There was a two-year period of time when he attended church once. He was too busy with his own interests to have an interest in me or the children. I prayed many hours about him and it just seemed God was not answering. Just when I thought he would respond, back he would step. I tried everything to get him to church. First I shamed him about shirking his fatherly responsibility; then I threatened to stay home when he wanted me to go with him unless he went with us. Thirdly, I bribed him. 'If you'll go with us, we'll fish with you all afternoon.' Nothing worked!"

She interrupted me, "That sounds exactly like us. What happened?"

"As I was praying for Rod, God was doing His work in me. I had been teaching submission in Sunday School and Bible studies since I was a teenager, and felt I was submissive. But God began bringing things to my attention to show areas where I was rebellious. The most influential was my study of Genesis in Bible Study Fellowship. There I found Sarah's submission to Abraham so great that even when he was wrong she revered him enough to call him lord. I realized I had never been truly submissive even when my actions looked like it. It had begun on the night of our wedding rehearsal. Rod's folks were there and his mother had very definite ideas of what we should do, and they conflicted with our plans. Rod agreed with his mother even though the change would be costly and would upset me. Our pastor jokingly said, 'You may want to omit "obey" from the ceremony.' At that moment I never wanted to obey him, so I said, 'I do want to drop it.' I forgot the whole incident until months later when Rod asked me to stay home from church with him. When I disagreed, he ordered me to obey him. Suddenly, I remembered I had not promised to obey in everything, so I went to church feeling very self-righteous about the whole situation. This was the pattern for our lives. I would do everything graciously that was asked or expected of me unless I thought it was improper, then I would refuse. When I saw what I was really like, I went to the Lord, confessed my rebellion, and asked for direction to correct my mistakes. In my mind I kept seeing Sarah kneeling before Abraham and knew I had to submit to Rod in everything, not only in what I chose to submit. I asked God to give me the courage to ask Rod's forgiveness. So on Sunday afternoon, I went into the front room where Rod was watching television and knelt down before Him, asked his forgiveness, and repeated my vows, including "obey." I wish I could say from that second on everything was rosy but I can't. I can say a process began that eventually led to Rod's active participation in our lives, including church. When asked what changed him, he talks of the difference he saw in me. In a nutshell, until I could show God's love in submission, I kept him from getting a clear picture of who God is. This is what God directed me to do. I don't know what He will ask of you."'

Later she shared that she had followed the same pattern and her husband had come to know Jesus as Saviour.

Some came with questions. One of the first asked was, "Why did God allow this to happen to her when there are all these little tramps walking around here?"

I answered, "But don't you see, if one of those little tramps, as you call them, had been taken, Satan would have won the victory, for they would have been forever out of God's reach. Our little girl knew God personally, and when she left her body, she went home. That other girl is still here where the Holy Spirit can draw her to God. This way even though Satan sought a victory, it belonged to God." I breathed a prayer, "Thank You, God, for his pain and questioning, for I heard Your answer from my own lips." Because we went to God quickly we had not thought of that, but I'm sure we would have later.

A woman came with anger in her heart against God. "How can I teach my children that God will take care of them as He promised after He has allowed such a terrible thing?"

I realized this would be one of the main questions in everyone's mind. As she continued her complaint against God, I remembered a time when I heard a Sunday School teacher end her story by having the children repeat after her, "If I love God, He will protect me and nothing bad will ever happen to me." Chills were going over me as I heard this same principle voiced. Could she not recall how God's people, all through the ages, had been killed? I sent an arrow prayer heavenward, "Help me, Lord, for I don't know the right words to say." I began, "I can only tell you what I believe, for it seems your belief is different than mine. Evil has been present in the world since Satan made his move to take control of the world from God, and evil will be with us until we reach the deadline God has set for us. During this period of time He never promised Christians they would be free from the effects of evil — in fact, quite the opposite. As long as we are not isolated from other people, we will be hurt by the sin spill-over. Now, He has promised to be with us in evil and always show us a way out of it when it is more than we can bear. This He did for Dana. He shared everything with her and then took her home to Himself since her innocence could not accept the evil lashed out at her. We even believe she was unconscious at the time and did not experience what went on with her body but Paul writes in Romans 8:18:

"For I reckon that the sufferings of this present time are not worthy to be compared with the glory which shall be revealed in us!"

"So, even if she did suffer, as have God's people since the beginning of time, she now can call it nothing. I'll admit I had some idea in the back of my mind that no child of God would ever be treated in this manner, but I had to realize that there was no such promise in the Scriptures. Also, I Peter 4:12 tells us:

"Beloved, think it not strange concerning the fiery trial which is to try you, as though some strange thing happened unto you."

"So we are not to be surprised at the kinds of evil that are turned on us but accept the fact that they will be on us until Christ returns and sets up His Kingdom to rule evermore." This explanation seemed to satisfy her and she left, at peace with God again.

I'm still amazed at how completely God controlled my emotions. It seemed important to Him for me never to lose control in public. Another amazing thing was the actual battle we could see and feel being waged by God and Satan. One incident will show what I mean about both.

On Wednesday afternoon, a young man newly called into the ministry, Roddy King, came to have prayer with us. He was then going to prayer meeting at Mayflower, where he was filling in for my father, the pastor, who was in revival at Waldo, Arkansas. As we began praying, I noticed a low murmur of children's voices and music in one of the bedrooms. I breathed, "Thank You, God, for this unusual time of quietness for us."

The prayers continued, with each of us, either verbally or silently, conversing with God, when suddenly my peace turned to anguish. The music had been turned up louder and the words being sung were, "Mama, I don't want to die. I sometimes wish I'd never been born at all." The music I was hearing was a recording of "Bohemian Rhapsody," the story of a boy who had killed someone and was to be executed. I had heard this song many times, but in my present condition, the boy's voice became Dana's voice calling, "Mama, I don't want to die . . ."

I felt myself screaming hysterically, "She's calling me. I have to get to her. O God, she's calling me, let me find her, don't let her die!" I could not pray or even think coherently, nor was I aware of anything that went on around me. The next time I was aware of anything, Rod was holding me and comforting me as I tried to tell him, between sobs, about it. As I tried to make him understand, into my mind came the thought that Satan was deliberately undermining my confidence in God. Since God had already told me Dana was with Him, I was just letting Satan scare me. The thought brought reason and calmness. "Thank You, God, for reminding me. I'm sorry I failed You — but bind Satan and don't allow him victory in my weakness."

Rod, by this time, grasped what I was telling him and said, "But honey, you never made a sound. We finished our prayer, and Roddy shook my hand and left. You were still sitting there with your head bowed as though praying. After the others left, you started sobbing like your heart was broken, but even then it was quiet. You didn't say anything until you started explaining to me. You were worried about nothing!"

I could not fully comprehend what he was saying until my sister reaffirmed it. "Thank You, Lord God, truly Your grace is sufficient for me and Your strength is made perfect in my weakness." (II Cor. 12:9)

Time passed. Friends came and went. One said, "I stay because I can only have peace when I'm here with you."

Another was passing through and stopped. "As I was driving, I seemed to be under a cloud of depression," she said. "Then when I was almost here, suddenly the depression lifted and I felt happy. The change was so great I had to stop and tell you. I know God is surrounding you with His love!" That is what we felt!

Around the clock volunteers answered the phone, accepted telegrams, and collected mail. Only when it was necessary would one of the family talk on the phone. It was beautiful how God worked even that simple task out for us. I could do nothing but cry if I was on the phone, but I could be calm otherwise. Renee would cry when talking in person but was perfectly calm on the phone. We each knew the area God wanted us to work for He gives the strength for the task He calls you to. By Thursday morning the total number of people reported praying for us reached 10,000. We quit keeping records but praised God for the loving concern of so many good people.

Of course, the FBI agents, the detectives, and the local law officers had to come to us for information and to make their reports. While these men showed us amazing consideration, still every conference was agony to me. It made me want to gather my children into my arms and protect them from all evil. The Lord really had to comfort me about that.

By Thursday afternoon, we were all thinking of nothing but that her body be found. There were absolutely no clues. One man, really concerned for us and trying to prepare us, said, "Sometimes they are never found."

I said nothing, but in my heart was a confidence that God would answer my prayer — my child's body would be found!

Another, who thought we had not recognized the total picture, said, "You do realize, if she is found, she could be naked or hurt badly."

"Yes," I said. "I do realize that." Feeling the need to pray again, I excused myself. I found Renee and my sister, Nancy, and shared with them my need for praying that Dana's body be found clothed. Not having the opportunity to pray together, we agreed to do it separately. I sought the quiet of my bedroom. "Dear Father, I come again into Your presence asking this purely selfish request. This is for Dana and me and doesn't matter to anyone else. You know how modest she was. Since she is alive and with You, she sees what is happening here. I believe, even in the body You've given her now, she would be shamed for her old body to be found unclothed. Lord, to hide her shame, and for my peace of mind, I petition You to have her body clothed. In Your Son's precious name I come, Amen."

Late Thursday night with everyone exhausted and no new leads to follow, the search teams were sent home to rest. When I realized they were quitting, I had a feeling of hopelessness. I felt they had given up hope of finding her. "Lord God, don't let them give up. I know You will show them where she is." Suddenly I realized how tired these people must be and was shamed into asking God's forgiveness about my attitude. Then I realized if I accepted God's word, she was with Him; time didn't matter. I had been trying to hold onto both hopes.

Recognizing our need for privacy, our friends left us with the promise of checking on us at intervals through the night. All the family went to bed and slept for a few hours. I was awakened by the song of a bird outside my window, and was amazed at how rested I felt. I lay still. "Thank You, Lord, for bringing me this quiet beauty before I have to face this day."

Then the memories came.

I remembered the good times we had shared as a whole family — the trips, games, jokes, church activities, family altar, so many memories.

I remembered how reluctant Dana had seemed to enter this world, being six weeks late; how purple she was as the doctor and nurses hurriedly tended her, thinking me unconscious on the delivery table; the relief all of us felt when she finally gave her first cry; the shock on the doctor's face when I asked, "Are all babies that color when they are first born?"

He assured me that all were not such a pretty color, but she would be all right. He then belatedly announced, "You are the mother of a big girl weighing twelve pounds, ten and one-half ounces."

Absurdly, I said, "She can't be a girl, she's too big!" Everyone laughed, and I knew she really would be all right.

I remembered the protective love shown her by her big brothers and sister, who watched carefully and told me when she started turning a little blue so I could elevate her feet, and the spoiling everyone gave her when we thought she would have surgery and the joy we shared when she did not.

I remembered the nickname the ladies in the lunchroom at school gave her: Little Angel. I worked in the library two days a week and she would go with me. When she became tired of books, she would visit the lunchroom and she became the workers' pet. The name stuck!

I remembered her as the school cheerleaders' mascot. How she always loved the sports activities! She thought she was as big as the regular cheerleaders and tried to do each cheer.

I remembered how excited she was about finally starting school. I also remember the fear that gripped me when she blacked out the first day and could not be revived for a time. There followed doctor calls, and hospitalization, with a verdict of epileptic seizures. We were told she would probably always have to avoid late nights, strenuous exercise, and undue excitement but might outgrow the need for medication. What joy we had when later the doctors let her omit the medicine!

I remembered when she had mononucleosis. We had no idea what was wrong and the hospital stay did not enlighten us. I would worry about her for she could not stay at school more than three hours a day, and then I would have to put her to bed for the rest of the day. Since I worked at the service station in the afternoons, I took a bed down there so I could take care of her. Two months later, we discovered the problem, but there was a long recuperative period.

I remembered the talent contests she entered at school. I saw her in her "Old Mop Woman" costume in front of a make-believe mirror doing a parody of "Wouldn't It Be Loverly?" and "I've Grown Accustomed To Her Face." Her only concern about being one of the winners was embarrassment because she would be taller than all but one of the escorts.

I remembered when only a month ago, she sang "I Believe in Miracles" in her clear, young voice, for Children's Church.

I remembered her being so proud of her father in the County Judge race. The night following his decision to run she made him a surprise — his first poster. We put it in the window at the service station. She also insisted on helping us work all night on two occasions silkscreening the other posters. In my mind's eye, I could still see her at 2 a.m. stretched out on a sleeping bag where she was going to rest a few minutes and then help us finish. On the bottom of her feet were letters where she had stepped on a wet poster. When Nancy, Renee, and I saw them, we had to smother our laughter, and she slept peacefully until morning.

I remembered our discussions about angels. She never had enough information about heaven and its occupants. One Sunday while the family was coming home from church, she asked, "Mother, how many angels did you say would come to help if someone were in trouble?"

"It doesn't say a special number, but God has multitudes He sends to carry out His will so you can bet as many as are needed will be there." She seemed satisfied.

I lay there with tears of remembrance wetting my pillow and my hair. Rod awoke and held me. We talked of her and the joy she brought to our lives. "Thank You, God, for those beautiful years."

TWO
Found

"And when he cometh home, he calleth together his friends and neighbors, saying unto them, Rejoice with me; for I have found my sheep which was lost."
Luke 15:6

Mid-morning there seemed to be a forced stillness among those around us. I realized that certain special friends were gathering around, the friends who would want to be with us when we most needed their strength. My heart seemed to swell, there wasn't enough room for it in my body. My throat ached and my vision kept blurring. I tried to be natural, but my mind had a life of its own. "I must act natural. They are trying so hard to pretend this is just another time, so I must not let them know I know. Dear God, can I take this? I know you've already told me she's with You, but this seems so final. Be strong in me, Lord. Please don't let me faint or be weak, for it will be even harder on the rest of the family if I do. Still my trembling, hold me tightly, Lord, for here they come."

The next time segment was like slides in a projector.

Bill Probasco, our pastor, came.

"They've found her body haven't they?" I asked.

"Yes," he sobbed, "I saw a body in the water with a pantsuit on like hers."

I heard nothing else he said. Over and over in my mind rolled the words, "body in the water with a pantsuit on like hers, body in the water with a pantsuit on like hers." It became a refrain in my mind.

Dr. Bob Banister, a friend and the county coroner, came along with several others, but he is the only one I remember. "It was Dana," he said, "I recognized her.

"She was fully clothed," he continued, "but she had been beaten. Do you want to know the whole thing? It's not pretty."

I roused myself enough to look at Rod, and then we nodded our assent. I let my refrain roll over in my mind again with his words playing in the background so as not to be so harsh.

"She had been beaten badly, having the lower flesh on her face completely severed from the bone but the bones and teeth were not broken. There were blue marks on her neck where she had been strangled. She had also been raped, but the actual death was caused by drowning after being put into a pond. She was probably unconscious most of the time, for there were no marks or scratches on her arms or wrists. There would have been if she had fought. I figure she probably died that Tuesday night before midnight, but there is no way to say for sure.

When God gave me the Scriptures, she was already with Him. Her body was found to comfort us, and even though the worst had happened to it, I knew she was unconscious. What a great God who prepared her in birth to meet death triumphantly! What a gently loving

God who allowed her body to be found fully clothed! One who would not let the boys find her body, though they had been within one-fourth mile of her twice. One who held the rain in His hand! God is so good to me!

When the officials came to inform us that they had recovered Dana's body, they found we already knew. They repeated the information, but I only partially listened.

Finally, we were given a few minutes of privacy so we could tell our sons and our daughter and shed our tears of relief that the search was over, and tears of sorrow that there would never again, in this lifetime, be a little girl who would fill the empty place in our heart and lives.

Two FBI agents came to tell us, "Since her body was found only eighteen miles from home, it now is out of our jurisdiction, but we want you to know some of us are staying on the case privately until something breaks. If we get reassigned, we'll take our vacation. Rest assured we will find the man who did this."

Praise belongs to You, Lord, for You are the only one who could give them that kind of love and devotion for us and the task before them.

I awoke early, yet refreshed, Saturday morning, with a feeling of urgency to complete the funeral details.

My parents were to come, and I was concerned for them. My children have always been like their children and this was especially true of Dana. I knew her death would be harder on them than anything they had ever faced before. My father, a minister, was away in a revival, and my mother was with him when we had to notify them that Dana was missing. We discussed the situation and decided they should continue with the work God had called them to do since there was nothing they could do here. We talked daily on the phone to give them the latest news and to see how they were doing. Each night at the services, there were special prayers said for Dana and us. After her body was recovered Friday, I knew they would want to join us and was concerned about them driving. Men from their church in Mayflower drove up to bring them home. I am proud to stand and say I serve a God with this kind of power, the power to enable someone to carry out His assigned task under this kind of strain. Praise God!

THREE
Prepare

*"Lord, thou hast heard the desire of the humble;
thou wilt prepare their heart, thou wilt cause thine
ear to hear."*
   Psalm 10:17

I dressed for our trip to the funeral home. Rod came in just as I began putting on my make-up. "Honey," I said, "would you find Dana's Bible and read the 103rd Psalm? Remember, it was the one she was memorizing."

He picked up her Living Bible. Opening it to the passage, he began to read:

"I bless the holy name of God with all my heart. Yes, I will bless the Lord and not forget the glorious things He does for me."

"That sounds just like her talking, doesn't it?" Rod said tearfully.

"It really does," I agreed and began the fight of tears versus make-up.

"He forgives all my sins. He heals me. He ransoms me from hell!"

"That assures us of her salvation," I interjected.

"He surrounds me with loving kindness and tender mercies. He fills my life with good things! My youth is renewed like the eagles!"

I remembered her lack of stamina. She never was as strong as our other children. Now she has all strength and stamina. She will never be limited by her body again.

"He gives justice to all who are treated unfairly!"

She was treated unfairly so the man will be caught and brought to justice. "Thank You, God. I'll hold onto that."

"He revealed His will and nature to Moses and the people of Israel. He is merciful and tender toward those who don't deserve it; He is slow to get angry and full of kindness and love. He never bears a grudge, nor remains angry forever. He has not punished us as we deserve for all our sins, for His mercy toward those who fear Him is as great as the height of the heavens, above the earth. He has removed our sins as far as the east is from the west. He is like a father to us, tender and sympathetic to those who reverence Him!"

I silently prayed, "I can see You holding her in Your loving arms, Father. Hold her for me."

"For He knows we are but dust, and that our days are few and brief, like grass, like flowers, blown by the wind and gone forever."

"Do you think she understood then that her life

would be short, or is it just in looking back that she sees God's plan?" I asked.

"I don't think she fully understood then, but it's for sure she does now," he replied. Then he continued:

"But the lovingkindness of the Lord is from everlasting to everlasting, to those who reverence Him; His salvation is to children's children of those who are faithful to His convenant and remember to obey Him!"

I realized more fully that she would experience only good from now through eternity.

"The Lord has made the heavens His throne; from there He rules over everything there is."

In my heart it seemed she was saying, "Mom, I know God rules over every circumstance, so I know He is in charge of this."

"Bless the Lord, you mighty angels of His who carry out His orders, listening for each of His commands. Yes, bless the Lord, you armies of His angels who serve Him constantly."

I remembered her excitement when we discussed angels who come to escort the dying home. Bro. Bill had a friend who, just prior to dying, saw four angels by his bed and knew they had come to take him home. Dana thought that was the "neatest thing!" "Thank You, Lord, for even as Your messengers came for her, she would know why they had come, so her departure was an exciting thing for her."

"Let everything everywhere bless the Lord. And how I bless Him, too!"

It seemed as though she said, "Mom, this is God's plan and I want you to know it's fine with me."

Rod and I both were openly crying now. My makeup was completely washed off, but there was a peace in my heart. We held each other and talked of how wonderful God is to let us know that Dana was prepared also. In this one passage God had told her her sins were forgiven, her life would be short, He would give justice, and His angels were at His command to come to her, and it ended as if Dana understood and, like Mary of old, said, "Be it unto me according to Thy word." Those beautiful words sustained us through the long weekend.

Rod, Mother, and I went to the funeral home to select the casket and cemetery plot. As soon as we walked through the door, I saw the casket I wanted — if it was within our price range. This same casket was selected individually by each of the three of us. Since it was also one of the more moderately priced ones, we felt God had helped us in our selection.

Then we went to the office to select the plot. While Rod was shown the available ones with their prices, I went to a wall sign that listed the different Gardens by name. I found one called "The Garden of Love." I thought, "She was the expression of our love for each other, she brought us love, and in love God took her home, so this is the place I want her."

Rod came and said, "Honey, the area having the most available plots, and therefore a cheaper rate, is the Garden of Love. Would that be all right?"

I smiled and nodded, not trusting my voice at that moment. We drove out to view it and found it perfect, as I knew it would be. "Thank You, Lord, that you can make the most trying situation a worship time. I have felt Your presence in a real way all morning. Thank you!"

Later, the seventh grade Sunday School class gave us a book entitled "Life Is Forever," by Helen Steiner Rice. In it is a poem entitled "The Tiny Rosebud God Picked to Bloom in Heaven" that seemed to confirm again our decisions that day in the funeral home.

We ran into a problem we had not anticipated when we started the financial arrangements for the funeral. We had secured burial plots, markers, etc. years earlier in Northwest Arkansas for the whole family. They were supposed to be transferable, but the local cemetery would not accept them and the original cemetery could not buy them back. Thus, our money was tied up. We knew where there is a need, God wants to fill that need so we prayed about it. We then decided to borrow the money, but God's plans are always larger than my expectations. God laid it on the hearts of the deacons in our church to provide for our financial needs. At first we were embarrassed that other people had assumed our debts, but God reminded me of Scriptures showing that we receive according to what we give. That did not only pertain to us but assured us that God would bless these special people over and over because they had given to us when we were in need. "Thank You, Lord, for the way You love and care for us through others. I ask You to pour out Your blessings on these beautiful men of Yours."

Parents do not expect their children to die before they do, so Rod and I had made out a service to be used when one or both of us died. Not liking the usual type of funeral for a Christian's home-going, we had planned a time of praise. Even though the present circumstances were not normal, we decided to use this same basic theme in Dana's service. We asked Bro. Bill to incorporate the two main scripture passages into the program for the text and Bro. Don Bingham to prepare the music around the praise theme ending with the Hallelujah Chorus. God had given us such spirit-filled and talented friends that we could rely on them to work out all the details, knowing it would all bring glory to God.

Because of the condition of Dana's body, we decided, as a family, not to view it. Well-meaning friends told us, "You can never really accept her death unless you see her." This wasn't true with us and we wanted to remember her in her sweet, young beauty.

When we read the Psalm passage earlier that day, I thought it was only for our comfort. I should have remembered God's character better than that. Until Saturday we had talked with adults wanting to know how we could bear our loss, but now it was young people who came to talk to us. They were not interested in how we stood it. What they wanted to know was how Dana could have endured such suffering and not blame God. This Psalm passage was what they also needed. When they learned she was prepared, probably unconscious, and comforted by angels who escorted her into God's presence, they left with their faith restored and strengthened.

Sunday morning came and I felt the need of fellowship with my church family. We decided not to attend Sunday School, for that would be so distracting, but we did attend worship service. I don't remember much of the message but I felt such a peace. My mind winged away to other times when we were all together in this special place. This was the first time I had sat down without feeling the need to share with someone since six-thirty Tuesday evening, so I felt incapable of productive thought. Then Bro. Bill mentioned the stoning of Stephen and how those around could tell by his countenance he was looking into the face of God. "This is what Dana experienced," I thought. "She was not feeling what went on with her body for 'she,' the part that is Dana, was already in the presence of God's glory, being ministered to by His angels."

Following the service, we visited a few short minutes with friends. One asked the question, "Why is it that you seem to accept Dana's death better than I do?" I shared a principle I learned earlier, through experience. The ones involved in the problem personally are given grace according to the problem. Others that are involved indirectly are not given as much. Therefore, when they allow themselves to become personally involved they are hurt.

Sunday afternoon and evening we shared with friends who visited us but did not attend worship services.

Dana (aged 11) just before a flower show: She loved flowers.

FOUR
Praise

"Make a joyful noise unto the Lord, all ye lands. Serve the Lord with gladness: come before his presence with singing. Know ye that the Lord He is God: It is He that hath made us, and not we ourselves; we are his people, and the sheep of his pasture. Enter into his gates with thanksgiving, and into his courts with praise: Be thankful unto Him, and bless His name. For the Lord is good; his mercy is everlasting; and his truth endureth to all generations.

Psalm 100:1-5

Monday came, the day of the funeral, and everything seemed normal and under control. Since we did not believe a Christian's home-going is a time of mourning but of rejoicing, we decided not to dress as if in mourning, choosing instead bright, happy clothes. Staying busy left me no time to think of the strain that was ahead of the family.

I was fine until we sat down in the car provided for the family. I became so tense I could not be still. Rod could tell how upset I was and, taking my hand, he kept a conversation going with the family that would keep our minds off the service ahead. The fifteen miles to the church seemed to stretch to one hundred fifteen! I would look away when we passed people standing by the road or when we met cars where the people craned their necks to get a better look at us. I felt our privacy had been invaded too much. Finally arriving, we were sitting quietly, waiting until time to go in, when suddenly I was overwhelmed with resentment at the presence of so many people. I would have liked to say goodbye to that precious body in private. "Lord," I silently prayed, "I know if this was not Your will, there would not be all these people here — but I'm not happy about it. I never dreamed there would be so many people. Help me to accept their presence as Your will and be able to praise You for their coming."

When I finished my prayer, Rod was saying, "Just look at all the people! Doesn't it just make you feel good? They have all hurt for us and this is their way of saying they care."

God filled my heart to overflowing with love for all those who had lined the roads, who filled the church, and the chapel, who were standing outside to listen to loudspeakers. "Thank You, Lord for being instant in answering prayers."

There were small incidents that almost shattered me. For instance, when we've gone anywhere as a family, we've always walked in three pairs, with Rod and myself, the girls, and then the guys. When we were walking down the aisle to our places, I realized Renee now had to walk alone. I couldn't bear for her to be by herself, so regardless of what it looked like, I reached back and had her come up and walk with us.

As we were seated, I looked at the closed casket that held the two special pictures we had framed for viewing. My sister had done the charcoal sketch for me while the search for Dana's body was still going on. It was a composite of several snapshots as well as remembered characteristics. It was Dana, even with the mischievous twinkle in her eye. A student from China who had visited our home the previous Christmas had taken the snapshot. It was typically Dana, with her long blonde hair in dog-ears, the funny grin on her face, and her new toe socks in gay colors showing out the front of her sandals.

The choir sang:

O, The Deep, Deep Love of Jesus

O, the deep, deep love of Jesus,
Vast, unmeasured, boundless, free!
Rolling as a mighty ocean
In its fullness over me.
Underneath me, all around me,
Is the current of Thy love;
Leading onward, leading homeward,
To my glorious rest above.

O, the deep, deep love of Jesus,
Love of ev'ry love the best!
'Tis an ocean vast of blessing,
'Tis a haven sweet of rest.
O, the deep, deep love of Jesus,
'Tis a heav'n of heav'ns to me;
And it lifts me up to glory,
For it lifts me up to thee."

Our minister, Bill Probasco, then began the service. "This is a service of worship in loving memory and recognition of the beautiful earthly life of Dana Diane Mize, who was born October 3rd, 1963, in Springdale, the daughter of Rodney and Jean Mize. Dana was a member of our congregation here at First Baptist Church and, left behind for their own pilgrimage through this life, hers having been finished, are her parents, Rod and Jean Mize, her brothers, Bill and Lance, her sister, Renee, and her grandparents, Mr. and Mrs. Herman Hurd and Mr. and Mrs. Charles Mize.

"For our comfort from God's Word, we want to consider the passage that God gave to Rod and Jean last week, and since it has been of such immense comfort to them we want to use it for our own comfort today. Isaiah 55:

> *Ho, everyone that thirsteth, come ye to the waters, and he that hath no money; come ye, buy, and eat; yea, come, buy wine and milk without money and without price. Wherefore do you spend money for that which is not bread? And your labour for that which satisfieth not? Hearken diligently unto me, and eat ye that which is good, and let your soul delight itself in fatness. Incline your ear, and come unto me: Hear, and your soul shall live; and I will make an everlasting covenant with you, even the sure mercies of David. Behold, I have given him for a witness to the people. Behold, thou shalt call a nation that thou knowest not, and nations that knew not thee shall run unto thee because of the Lord thy God, and for the holy one of Israel; for he hath glorified thee. Seek ye the Lord while He may be*

found, call ye upon Him while He is near: Let the wicked forsake his way, and the unrighteous man his thoughts: and let him return unto the Lord, and He will have mercy upon him: and to our God, for He will abundantly pardon. For My thoughts are not your thoughts, neither are your ways My ways, saith the Lord. For as the heavens are higher than the earth, so are My ways higher than your ways, and My thoughts than your thoughts. For as the rain cometh down, and the snow from heaven, and returneth not thither, but watereth the earth, and maketh it bring forth and bud, that it may give seed to the sower, and bread to the eater: So shall My word be that goeth forth out of my mouth: It shall not return unto Me void, but it shall accomplish that which I please, and it shall prosper in the thing whereto I sent it. For ye shall go out with joy, and be led forth with peace: the mountains and the hills shall break forth before you into singing, and all the trees of the field shall clap their hands. Instead of the thorn shall come up the fir tree, and instead of the brier shall come up the Myrtle tree: and it shall be to the Lord for a name, for an everlasting sign that shall not be cut off.

"Let's pray together. Our Father, we take such comfort in Thy word, for this life is most surely a life of uncertainty as far as human beings are concerned. We simply do not know one moment to the next, nor does our right hand know what our left hand does. We have no more certainty than a staggering man going forth into the darkness not knowing where he is. But, O Father, You have given us Your Word. It is our lamp and our light. It is our strong standard and infallible witness not only of Thy love but of Thy purpose for our being here. Help us never to forget, Lord, that a person's life is not measured by You in terms of length as men know length but in terms of quality as only God the Spirit ministering the holy life of Jesus within us can give that life. We come today to thank You for the years You gave us with Dana, and we come to thank You especially that she took Christ as her Saviour and made Him her Lord. Because of the out-living of the Christ life she was beautiful in our midst. Do grant, our Father, Your strength and comfort to the family and the many friends and gather our thoughts together now, Lord, and our emotions, may they be held back for a moment, while we consider Thy Word together for Jesus' sake, Amen."

We, along with the congregation, joined the choir and sang a praise hymn, "All Hail the Power of Jesus' Name." I found real joy in voicing my praise.

George Duke, my brother-in-law, then sang:

My Tribute, To God Be The Glory

How can I say thanks for the things
    You have done for me?
Things so undeserved, yet you gave
    to prove Your love for me.
The voices of a million angels could
    not express my gratitude.
All that I am, and ever hope to be,
    I owe it all to Thee!
To God be the glory,
To God be the glory,
To God be the glory

For the things He has done.
With His blood He has saved me,
With His power He has raised me,
To God be the glory for the things
   He has done.
Just let me live my life, let it
   be pleasing Lord, to Thee,
And should I gain any praise,
   let it go to Calvary.
With His blood He has saved me,
With His power He has raised me,
To God be the glory for the things
   He has done.

Brother Bill gave forth the message God laid on his heart. Here is a portion of that message:

"There are a lot of people who would not understand why Christians could come to a memorial service and sing 'To God Be The Glory' and there are a good many people who do not understand, Rod and Jean, the control and confidence which you have exuded along with the boys and Renee and the rest of the family, during this awful time and during the ordeal of waiting. As I've already said to the congregation, last week our Lord gave you our text for today. After reading it carefully and prayerfully, you came to conclude that through it the Lord was telling you that Dana had been taken from you, and yet at the same time, this agonizing act would not in any way alter God's promises. He told you through this that she was at peace and with Him, and moreover, that He would get Himself glory, not in the sordid crime, but over it. Therefore, He accomplished two things in permitting it. He had gathered Dana to Himself, for He has the prior claim. Yours is a claim to her by natural birth but His is by the new birth. And moreover, He would use Satan's evil rage to Satan's disadvantage. The entire affair would have the effect of calling attention to the grace and glory of Jesus Christ by showing that His grace is greater than sin and His power greater than death.

This nightmarish ordeal will be used to call attention, as sure as God is living, it will be used to call attention to His undeserved grace and bring many to heed His loving call.

'Seek ye the Lord while He may be found, call ye upon Him while He is near. Let the wicked forsake his way, and the unrighteous man his thoughts: and let him return unto the Lord, and He will have mercy upon him; and to our God, for He will abundantly pardon. For My thoughts are not your thoughts, neither are your ways My ways, saith the Lord.'

"We are furthermore reminded by Isaiah that although we cannot understand God's ways, we can certainly predict them from God's Word. For He has not left us in this world to try to speculate as to what His ways are and why His ways are that way. The written Word of God is God's message to men telling man what God is doing in this present world. God's purposes in this present world are carefully documented within that Word and the Word gives absolutely no doubt but that God is presently moving all things toward that appointed day in which He will fully and finally restore man and this earth back to His rule and bring all of the fallen creation, both man and material, back to Himself.

Now these purposes take time to unfold; and time, of course, means that human life is being lived out. Whether we like it or not, we have to face the awful consequences of our sin. We have to live that life out in the environment created by that sin. God, being just, must allow human life to go on in its fallen state for a time until the entire course of human life originally planned has been fulfilled.

"God's eye is good, my friend. Although we do not as yet know who did this sickening deed, God does. He watched it, just as He watched the violence and corruption continue to plunge His peaceful Eden into horror, just as He watched Cain rise up against his brother, Abel. But at the same time He tells us, 'Vengeance is mine, I will repay.' When it is purposeful in view of His purposes for this earth, He will make known through the means appointed in human government who it was who did it, and if it should be that He never shows us, make no mistake about it, the deed will not go unpunished. But at the same time we must remember that God has a higher purpose than vengeance.

"God's angels, anxious as they were to prevent all of this, enraged with righteous indignation at what their horrified eyes were seeing, straining to smite the wretch, just as they smote Sodom and Gomorrah, were restrained by the Lord from doing so. Instead they were dispatched upon a more glorious mission — to escort Dana, in the light of her risen Lord, into the palace of the Most High, there to have her first audience in His immediate presence. And if she suffered, and if she was afraid, and if her innocent mind could not comprehend the anger and cruelty of her demon-possessed abductor, it was all swallowed up on the glorious appearing of her

Lord to receive her to Himself; and just as godly Stephen died, not with the pain of the stones but with the glory of the Lord upon his face, so all of God's saints who live near him can count on that blessed presence when it's time to be summoned out of this world.

"Her captor, therefore, unwittingly became her releasor, not confining her, as he thought, to his own satanic will, but becoming the means by which her precious spirit broke its bonds and soared into the arms of her Father and her God, her Saviour and her Lord, and into the presence of saints and angels from time immemorial. For a time her washed soul, having been cleansed in the blood of Christ, must take her place beside the altar to ask with the martyred saints of the ages,

> *'How long O Lord, Holy, and True, Dost Thou not avenge and judge our blood on them that dwell upon the earth?'*

"And her Savior takes her gently into His lap, as He did the children of another day, wiping her tears away; and He summons a strong angel to give her a white robe and let her rest a little season, until we too have resisted unto blood, striving against sin, and then we shall join her.

"Meanwhile, she is being given her first lesson in higher eschatology, viewing from a heavenly perspective the final fulfillment of His will, as the Lord appoints Moses, or King David, or John, or Paul, or Augustine, or Spurgeon to show her the glorious things which shall come to pass hereafter.

"Do you realize that the only way God can allow the world to continue as it is now is to give it enough grace to overcome all that sin and death can do? While He allowed it to be subjected to vanity, He subjected it to hope in Jesus Christ and in this age of grace, even by this thing that has been done, He will use it to bring someone to Himself. I wonder — could it be you? Could it be you who are saying, 'I wish I had that hope?' You can. The same one who gave it to this family will give it to you in Jesus Christ.

"And now, Father, we have delivered the message You have given us. We have not come here to eulogize, we have come to rejoice. We thank You for this little girl, this precious child who represents for all of us the beauty, the brightness, the blessing of godly children. Were it not for our Lord, we would be enshrouded at this moment in a cloud of gloom, but our Saviour, You, in rolling the stone away, rolled away our gloom, and we come to say the Lord God Omnipotent reigneth, hallelujah, In Jesus' name. Amen."

The Sanctuary Choir then sang "The Hallelujah Chorus" from Handel's Messiah.

I felt so exultant as I listened to that beautiful song of praise that I thought the whole family of God would be raptured!

We waited inside the car before the church for what seemed ages but I didn't mind now, for I was able to see the beautiful people who had shared the worship experience with us. Later we found there had been 1,126 people who signed our Memorial book. I was especially comforted to find I knew all but eight of them. They were not just curiousity seekers but friends who loved us and wanted to show that love.

We waited again at the gravesite for the three-mile-long procession to arrive. We watched as a car door was shut on a friend's thumb. She calmly wrapped it in a handkerchief and took her place so as not to cause a distraction in the service. We knew she had probably broken it and was in intense pain. I silently prayed, "Thank You, Lord, for giving her the ability to accept her pain in this manner."

One of the things I remember most about the gravesite was the profusion of beautiful flowers. I almost requested no flowers be sent, but I knew many would want to express their love in this manner, so I relented. Besides, one of Dana's talents was a green thumb. She loved flowers and when mine would wilt, she would say, "Let me fix them for you." Somehow they would begin to grow. I know she must have enjoyed the floral display.

The services at the gravesite were very simple. Bro. Bill read the 103rd Psalm and voiced the prayer. It was necessary for us to leave immediately afterward so the large number of friends could depart.

We revisited the site later in the afternoon for our private goodbye. I selected one flower from each spray and all the potted plants to take home. The flowers filled the house and their fragrance was strong and sweet.

FIVE
Time

"To everything there is a season, and a time to every purpose under the heaven: a time to be born, and a time to die; a time to plant, and a time to pluck up that which is planted; a time to kill, and a time to heal; a time to break down, and a time to build up; a time to weep and a time to laugh; a time to mourn, and a time to dance; a time to cast away stones, and a time to gather stones together; a time to embrace, and a time to refrain from embracing; a time to get, and a time to lose; a time to keep, and a time to cast away; a time to rend, and a time to sew; a time to keep silence, and a time to speak; a time to love, and a time to hate; a time of war, and a time of peace."
Ecclesiastes 3:1-8

In the early evening following the services, we had a quiet Bible reading and prayer time. The chapter for our family to read that day was Proverbs 11. I was filled with thankfulness as Rod read to us from the Living Bible. The entire chapter showed God's justice and how the evil man always perishes but the good are lifted up. My favorite was verse 21,

"You can be very sure that the evil man will not go unpunished forever. And You can also be very sure that God will rescue the children of the godly."

God had already promised to bring justice but this was a timely reassurance. We discussed the lack of clues with confidence, knowing that God knew their location and would unveil them in His time.

That evening I felt a deep need for sleep. I had already said goodnight to Lance, Bill, and Renee, when my untrained mind led me to the girls' room to say goodnight to Dana. When I saw the bed, I remembered. The longing for her was so intense I fell to my knees and cried, "Dear God, help me! I want to hold and kiss my little girl so much it hurts. Just one more time, Lord. Just one touch. How can I bear to never touch her again?" The tears flowed and seemed to wash my eyes clear so I could see my own selfishness. "Lord, I'm sorry. You know I would never wish her back into this evil world for a minute, but I miss her so much! I can't touch her, Lord, but You can. Would You kiss her goodnight for me?" I stood up and, with a peaceful heart, went to bed.

The next several days were busy, with friends calling on us.

With the papers full of polygraph tests, reward money, and odd rumors, we could not keep our mind away from Dana's death.

One day we were told it was necessary to exhume Dana's body. Maybe, because of the long period of emotional upheaval, I was more susceptible, but this was much worse for me than the burial. I could hardly bear the idea of her body being touched again. I had to reason with myself.

"I know that body is precious to God, for it housed the Holy Spirit as well as Dana's 'self' while she was here. Later, God Himself will raise it up, change it, and reunite it with her 'self' which has been with Christ. Therefore, that body is important! But God also can, and will, gather the scattered parts of bodies and reunite them and change them so this should not be a problem."

The day of Dana's funeral God gave us a Scriptural promise that He would bring her murderer to justice but time was passing and there seemed to be no clues. I was depressed and asked the Lord why He wasn't doing anything. I had become fearful that the promise might mean at the time of judgment rather than now.

On a particularly low day my Scripture reading was Habakkuk I. As I began reading it, I found in verses 2-4 that Habakkuk was voicing my feeling. "O Lord, how long shall I cry, and thou wilt not hear! even cry out unto thee of violence, and thou wilt not save! Why dost thou shew me iniquity, and cause me to behold grievance? for spoiling and violence are before me: and there are that raise up strife and contention. Therefore the law is ignored and judgment doth never go forth: for the wicked doth compass about the righteous; therefore justice comes out perverted." But more important in verse 5 Habakkuk gave me a new promise from God. "Behold ye among the heathen, and regard, and wonder marvelously: for I will work in your days, which ye will not believe, though it be told you." How I praised the Lord! Here He promised that He was going to do the work He had promised in my day and in a manner which would be unbelievable.

From then on I never doubted the man would be caught and brought to justice. I knew it would be in my lifetime even though it might look as if it was an impossible task.

But I still did not want her body disturbed. We suggested alternatives but were assured it was necessary. We gave our consent.

The day we went to the court house to sign the release papers, I was so weak and shaky I had to continually send thought prayers up for physical strength. We signed the papers, assured Judge Roberts personally that this was our wish, and left. I dropped Rod off at work and went home to bed with a migraine. I prayed, "O, Lord, I cannot believe the pressure I feel. I can tell it won't leave until this whole thing is settled. Lord, I can't be strong anymore. Please, give me a rest and a time to draw closer to you. In Jesus' name, Amen."

As we tried to go back to a normal routine, the investigation continued.

On April 25th Lt. Ken McFerran of the Criminal Investigation Section of the Arkansas State Police and Joe Martin, Faulkner County Sheriff, followed a lead to an undisclosed eastern state. We were told it was a firm lead so we were full of suppressed inquiry.

Since it was only a month until the primary election, we felt we had to go on with our part of the campaign. Our friends were divided with their advice. One group thought it improper to be involved like that so soon after Dana's death and the other group thought we should not allow her death to influence us. In trying to make our decision, we fell back on a never-fail principle: If God leads you into something, stay there until He leads you out! He had definitely led Rod to enter so here we would stay. Following that decision, another problem came up: should we have a low-key program or go all out? Our basic nature was to go all out, but trying not to offend, we were considering the alternative until we realized the other candidates, out of courtesy, could only do what we did. So we jumped in and began work again. I am so thankful for this work. I'm sure we needed to stay so busy we didn't have time to wonder about other things.

On April 28th, John Elliott Gruzen pleaded not guilty to the charge of murder in Union County Court in Elizabeth, N.J. and was held at Trenton State Prison. He was 5'7" tall, weighing 135 lbs., with reddish-brown long hair and beard. He lived at home with his parents, Mr. and Mrs. Benjamin Gruzen, was 33 years old and unmarried. He had been arrested at Fair Oaks Hospital, a center for persons with psychiatric problems, where he had admitted himself on the 16th. With an IQ of 137, he was a recent honor graduate of Rutgers State University in Brunswick, N. J., with degrees in psychology and sociology. It was reported he was a photographer but without regular employment.

It was hard to express our feelings at that point. As a family, we discussed our surprise at the absence of anger or hatred. I have felt more anger at a teacher who reacted unwisely to one of my children than I felt for this man I was sure had murdered my daughter. I did feel relief that he was caught so no one else need be killed, and thankful it was not a local person, for that could have hurt so many people I knew and loved. One of our friends, talking about this strange phenomenon, said, "It will probably be different when you see him. He's not a real person to you yet." I was afraid that might be true, so I took it to the Lord that night. "O, Lord, I guess this man isn't real to me yet — or I may be in shock — but I ask You, please be with us and control us. Give us Your reactions so we will act only in a way that will bring glory to Your name. I pray for the Gruzen family. It is so much worse for them than for us. Lift them up and draw them to You for comfort. I also pray for him. He has to be filled with evil to do this deed, so I pray You will reveal Yourself to him. It seems You could have even more glory if this man came to a saving knowledge of You. Lord, help us to be examples of Your forgiving love. I pray our attitudes might not be temporary but the true ones You have given us as You have given them in the past. Lord, I give all this to You, asking that Your will be done in Jesus' name. Amen."

Gruzen pleaded mental incompetency on May 5th to fight extradition, and a hearing was set for June 7th.

In the meantime, the campaign was coming to the final days. We had changed our tactics so I could be more useful. I originally was to go out and meet people like Rod did but that did not work for me. After the third house, I was in such an emotional state, I quit. When these dear people found out who I was, they were so hurt, all they could do was cry. When other people cry, I usually do also, so it didn't take long to use up my emotional stamina. In fact, for a while I didn't want to go anywhere. Twice when we went into a restaurant to eat, people began to weep. In view of this unforeseen situation, we decided I could use the phone and manage the headquarters more effectively. Rod met nearly every family in Faulkner County.

We felt optimistic about the response we were receiving. Not wanting sympathy votes, we encouraged everyone to look at the qualifications of the candidates and vote for the one best fit for the office. Each time we had prayer, we asked God to direct us to the people He wanted to vote for us. As we talked to someone, it was exciting to wonder, "Are you one of the ones chosen to vote for us?"

May 25th, the day of the primaries, finally came. Headquarters was decorated; guests were invited; radios, score sheets, and pencils were everywhere; volunteers were ready to be at the polling places; and we were as excited as if this was a presidential position. When we gathered for our prayer time that day, Rod prayed, "Lord, we have done everything we know to do. I thank You for the warm reception I've had in this race and for the good people You've given us to show us what to do. Now we leave everything in Your hands. You can place in the minds of those special ones a desire to vote for me. I thank You for them. In Jesus' name, Amen."

The waiting began, but we were used to waiting. The first returns that came in were from the Conway area and we won a large margin. Everyone was cheering and excited. Everyone except me. I called my sister off to the side and said, "I don't think Rod can make it. This was our best area, and we don't have a large enough lead. Pray for God's will, but if it is not God's will for Rod to win, he will be crushed. We've had to believe he might win in order to do our best. Pray that Rod can accept God's will even if it means we lose."

We went back to our table to tally scores and tried to act as if the win was sure. As the other precincts called in, our lead dwindled more and more until it was obvious we had lost. My heart broke when I looked at Rod. He had a stunned expression on his face. I could almost hear him say, "Lord, I've done everything You asked me to, now why haven't You done Your part?" I felt at a loss to know what to say to him, so I just tried to be beside him to give my support. As he congratulated the two who would be in the run-off, he was very composed and gracious. After everyone had made comments, trying to lessen the hurt, Dad led us in prayer, and a tired group began to disperse. For over two months we had been through every emotion imaginable and suddenly we felt the load of each of them. We were completely exhausted! I asked each one to remember us in daily prayer, for I could tell we would need it.

It was even harder, now, to try to get back in a normal routine, for we had been in the public eye so much we had become a tourist attraction. So many people came, some with problems, some out of curiosity, and some were open enough to say they wanted to be able to say they had touched us. Some old customers came to the station as they were passing through and would ask about Dana, not knowing she was gone. It finally became a chore for any of us to go to work at the service station. We hunted for any excuse to close it. Rod took another job, but the publicity went on.

SIX
Trial

"That the trial of your faith, being much more precious than of gold that perisheth, though it be tried with fire, might be found unto praise and honour and glory at the appearing of Jesus Christ."
    I Peter 1:7

On June 7th, a sanity hearing was held for Gruzen in New Jersey, where it was ruled he was "competent and aware of legal proceedings," though suffering from chronic schizophrenia. Thus, he was brought to Arkansas and committed to the Arkansas State Hospital for 30 days' observance. Following this period there were differences in opinion with the prosecutor, Alex Street, asking for an additional period. This was denied but a sanity hearing was scheduled for November 2nd.

As each examination progressed, we heard the comments, "He'll never be brought to trial," or, "He'll get off completely free," but we knew God's promise and held on to it. This was a time when our faith was on trial also.

In the sanity hearing, Judge Roberts found Gruzen

competent to stand trial and assist his attorney in his defense, but he did agree to a change of venue. The trial was set for Feb. 9, 1977 in Danville, Ark. in Yell County.

It was a very emotionally exhausting experience for us to sit during the hearing and listen to testimony that was trying to keep the man we were sure had killed our daughter from coming to trial. We had to pray for strength and God's will to be done.

I looked at the Gruzen family and realized what a terrible thing this must be for them. When the decision was made for him to stand trial, we filed out of the courtroom as quickly as we could without causing comment. I was prepared to shout a "Praise the Lord," but Rod touched my arm and motioned toward some TV cameras that were aimed at us. I smothered my outburst of joy and we walked quietly to the car. A block away we finally could relax and show our joy.

On Feb. 7th a pretrial hearing was held to suppress evidence but the motion was denied.

With much trepidation we prepared to attend the trial. Rod and Bill were to testify the first day of questioning and since it would be easier on them to be familiar with the procedures and people involved, we wanted them to be there early. I wanted to know how the law officials found out John Gruzen had murdered Dana, and I was not sure I would ever know the full truth unless I was there, so I chose to attend. On the negative side, I knew there would be reporters and curious people and was not sure how well I could take being in the public eye so openly. Renee and I decided the answer would be to stay busy, so we took needlework, books, crossword puzzles, and notebooks. Nancy, an artist, took her sketch pad and effectively kept our minds diverted during the three long days of jury selection.

A lovely Christian family, the McCormicks, invited us to share their home. We gratefully accepted, with the family members taking turns staying there, in order that everyone did not have to go back and forth each day.

The fourth morning, just prior to court beginning, Rod called the immediate family into a small room for a family conference. Brother Bill joined us. Rod then told us, "They've just told me they have some evidence they may need to present that could be very upsetting to the family. I've already given our consent for it to be used, but I felt you should be prepared for it. It is her hands. They may be presented as evidence."

My stomach had already been tense, but at the actual words, I felt such a pain I thought I would be sick. I looked at the others. They, like me, looked unperturbed, but I knew how they felt inside and sent up an arrow prayer, "Lord, help us!"

We discussed whether we should stay if they presented this evidence and decided we would. We then commited this to God as well as the testimony Rod and Bill were to give.

Returning to the courtroom, I saw my parents and Rod's parents. I knew that they could not bear it if Dana's hands were used in evidence. I went to them and tried to get them to go home but they felt the need to be present also. Rod's sister, Conye Johnson, had come with his parents, so I took her aside and told her what problem was. She agreed to take them out immediately if we thought it necessary. Nancy agreed to do the same with Mom and Dad. As we awaited proceedings, I felt relaxed until the defense attorney requested Bill, not

Rod, to wait outside instead of with the family. My first thought was, "You rotten Shammus!" My second thought was that the first one was my real feeling toward this lawyer, so I would have to pray for my attitude toward him. "Lord, what a thin skin I have that such a small incident could shake me. I'm sorry, and I pray for this man whose actions stir me so quickly to anger. Give me a love for him that is greater than the remarks he will make. I pray for Bill, for he doesn't have the family support. Please be with him. Thank You, Lord, for being there. In Jesus' Name, Amen."

The prosecution presented the defendant's movements from the time he left New Jersey until his return:

April 8, 1976 — He left home, arriving in Little Rock at 1:17 p.m. His mother reported him missing. He rented a 1976 silver-gray Malibu and checked in at the Alamo Plaza Motel.

April 9, 1976 — He began the hunt for a gun, going to two places where he was turned down, being an out-of-state visitor.

April 10, 1976 — He tried to buy a gun from "Square Deal" in Little Rock, and when they refused, he paid a man to buy one for him from that establishment.

April 11, 1976 — Mrs. Gruzen notified New Jersey police that she had heard from her son in Tennessee. He claimed to be a movie director hunting secluded areas for a film.

April 12, 1976 — He moved to Conway at the King's Inn.

April 13, 1976 — He asked the desk clerk for directions to Vilonia.

April 14, 1976 — He checked out of the King's Inn.

April 15, 1976 — He drove to Oklahoma City, turned in his car, and took Amtrack to New Jersey.

April 16, 1976 — Arriving, he contacted his psychiatrist and had himself admitted into Fair Oaks Hospital, where he related to him, in detail, the crime which he had committed.

Dr. Puzin then called Dr. Revitch and they decided the crime was probably real. Dr. Revitch then called Captain Ballatt to see if there was such a crime in Arkansas.

April 22, 1976 — Mrs. Revitch called Mrs. Gruzen, telling her that John was in trouble. When Mrs. Gruzen questioned her, Mrs. Revitch referred her to Ballatt. Mrs. Gruzen then called Capt. Ballatt to find out what trouble her son was in but he did not know. Then Lt. Richard Mason put these two separate items together, called Arkansas and confirmed the crime, made a search of the Gruzen home, and arrested John Gruzen.

Rod and Bill did well on the witness stand. Even though I could tell they were a little nervous, they answered with clarity and calmness.

One of the things I wanted, once the trial started, was to see the pictures taken of Dana when her body was found. It became an obsession with me. I was the only one who wanted to do this, but Rod refused to allow me to see them. I know God leads Rod to make the correct decisions for me, so I prayed, "Lord, You know I have this desire to see those pictures and You also know Rod has said I can't. If it is not Your will for me to see them, please remove the desire. But, Lord, if You will permit this, please change Rod's mind. I await Your will, in Jesus' name. Amen."

I am continually amazed at how God works!

Just prior to the presentation of these pictures to the jury, there was a break and all the family, except me, was wandering around. I had a touch of flu and only wanted to sit still. The prosecutor held the pictures in his hand, behind his back, and when he turned his back to the audience, I was able to see her. This was God's way! Not close up, where the harsh facts would be forever imprinted on my mind, but from across the courtroom where I could still recognize her. From there she only looked disheveled and perhaps asleep. I was facinated by her hands, for they lay as I had seen them so often when she slept. My eyes filled, but my cold could account for my red nose and eyes, and my heavy use of the tissues. I prayed, "Thank You, precious Lord! Your ways truly are not my ways. As usual You found another way to meet my needs other than the one I had suggested. I praise You for who You are, In Jesus' name, Amen."

The Scripture in Matthew 10:30 that says,"But the very hairs of your head are all numbered" became real to me in a new way. The first time I heard the explanation, that God didn't mean He knew the total number of hairs on your head but that each hair had a specific number known to Him, I thought, "How wonderful!"

Then when one of Dana's hairs was presented as evidence to help prove she had been in this specific car, I could almost picture God saying, "That's number 72,142," or some other number. The witness then stated that the hair had not been pulled out but had fallen out of its own accord. This was more precious for it was as though God said, "Hair number 72,142, it is time for you to be useful, disembark." That Scripture will always be most special to me!

When the prosecution finished it's presentation of evidence, I realized he had not produced Dana's hands. Again we were reminded God would not allow more than we could stand. We thanked and praised Him that He spared us this, for of ourselves we cannot see how we could have stood it.

The defense attorney dwelt on Gruzen's past history of psychological problems.

After a full seven days of giving testimony, the jury took thirty-five minutes to bring a verdict of guilty and, after deliberation, recommended life in prison without pardon or parole.

God had been faithful! It was stated in the papers as a "one in a million chance" for him to be caught. We knew it was God using men to reveal the clues, in His time. Many had said, "He'll never make it to trial, and if he does, they'll let him off." Praise God, He is faithful!

I was so relieved that everything was settled so we could go home. Renee, Bill, and Lance rode home with Nancy, and Rod and I came home together. As we left

Danville, I said, "There's only one thing I regret about this whole business. I would have liked to say something to the Gruzens. That would neatly settle everything."

Rod agreed, and we drove on. Since we were both tired, he suggested we drink a cup of coffee at Russellville, so we stopped at a restaurant. We ordered and had just been served when in walked the Gruzen family. We were discussing the best way to approach them when Mrs. Gruzen walked up to our table. "You can't know how sorry we are about your little girl. We have a daughter also, so we can imagine how terrible it must have been for you."

"Thank you. I know it must be even harder on your family than on us," I assured her. "We have and will continue to pray for you."

We wished each other happier times, and she returned to their table. I could only look at Rod and say, "Thank You, Lord." The Scripture came to mind in Philippians 1:6:

> *"Being confident of this very thing, that He which hath begun a good work in You will perform it until the day of Jesus Christ."*

I should have known God would not leave anything undone. I had a feeling of completeness, of having finished my task.

Years before, I had to acknowledge that I was a person who could be strong under fire but afterward I would let down. When a child was ill, I was strong; but when that child became well, I would collapse. I had learned to watch myself so I would avoid this situation. I would love to be able to say I did not allow this to happen now, but the opposite was true.

True, I had the flu so I was not physically up to par, and true, these were unusual circumstances. My natural man gave me all kinds of reasons that I should be allowed a rest, and I agreed with them all, but this was not to be. In my own obstinate way, I began a period of rebellion. I didn't rant and rave against God; I decided to ignore Him. I knew He would not use a dirty or empty vessel, so I became both. For two weeks, I refused to read my Bible or say a prayer. Not one person called me, not one person came to see me, nor did I receive any written communication. I read, I sang, I listened to records, I slept, I did anything I wanted to do. The strange thing was that I constantly felt God's presence, almost as if He were hovering over me, isolating me from everything. I knew with certainty that when I wanted to reach Him, He would be there. I could not comprehend such love! The morning came when I woke up with a strong desire for fellowship with God again. With a broken heart, I confessed my waywardness and rebellion and asked His forgiveness. I was given another view of His grace. He knew my limits and gave me that rest I desired. What shames me is, had I not been in rebellion, but waited on Him, He would have given it to me and I would have had no regrets. What a blessing I missed in not being triumphant in that period of time!

Shortly after this period I began having a recurring dream that came two or three times a month. It always began with me asleep in bed. The doorbell would ring. I would get out of bed, put on a robe, and go to the door. When I opened it, Dana would be standing there. She was cold and dirty, and older than when she was killed. As I would stand there in surprise looking at her, she would begin crying and say, "I've been lost for so long.

Why haven't you been looking for me?" I would reach for her only to awaken with empty arms and tears streaming down my face. I realized Satan was working on my subconscious mind in order to weaken my faith and give me doubts concerning Dana's death. I took the problem to the Lord several times but the dream kept returning.

I knew that sometimes there is within a person an unconscious refusal to accept the death of a loved one and it would manifest itself in this way. I was ashamed to find this weakness in me after all the beautiful things God had done. I could not talk about it for a time. Then one day I shared it with the family, only to find some of them were having a similar problem. We began praying for each other and sharing this part of our lives with others who had lost loved ones. The dreams left and we rejoice in the peace that has replaced them.

As I sit here in retrospection upon this memorable year, I can see God's hand even more. Truly His thoughts were not our thoughts, neither were His ways our ways, for His ways were higher than our ways and His thoughts higher than our thoughts.

One of my favorite sayings is:

"Peace and joy are twin blessings of the gospel. Peace is joy resting and joy is peace dancing."

I have experienced both this year, according to His promise in Isaiah, even when there did not appear to be anything to be joyful about.

He has allowed us the privilege, not only of seeing spiritual growth in our own family but also of seeing other lives change.

I commit this writing to Him knowing that everything we do in His will will accomplish whatever He wants it to accomplish and will not return void. I hope you can see the sufficiency of my Lord and Saviour and if you do not know Him personally, that you would choose to do that today.

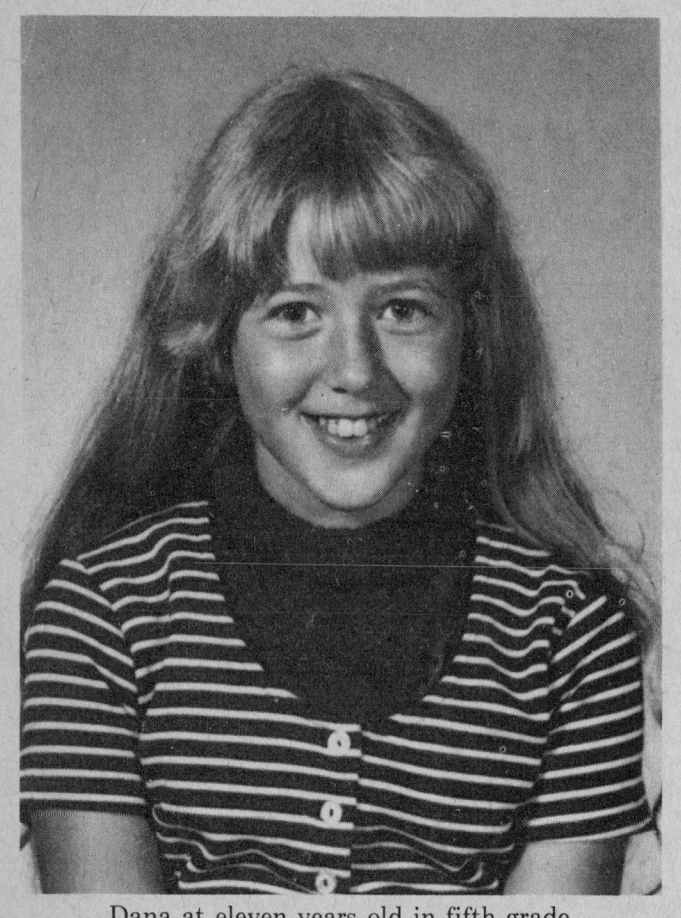

Dana at eleven years old in fifth grade.

Renee, Dana, Lance and Bill. This is the last family picture taken before Dana's death.

Epilogue

I want to share some of our beliefs about grief and why we did not outwardly grieve as some do.

What is grief? According to Webster's Dictionary, it is intense emotional suffering caused by loss, or a feeling of deep, acute sorrow.

Everyone who suffers loss experiences grief. The manner in which it is handled is where we differ. God made each of us a separate entity. We are unique physically, temperamentally, and ethnically. The different combinations of these help influence our actions.

Also, there are crossroads we come to and our choices determine what our reactions will be.

The first crossroad is whether we accept the death of Jesus Christ, God's Son, for our sins, which means He's our Savior. If we do not accept this, we have only our own resources to call upon in the time of grief. If we accept Him, we have all the resources of God to sustain us!

Another crossroad that Christians face is Jesus' Lordship. Do we say, "Thank You, Lord, for being my Saviour but now I can run my life," or "Lord, You created me, and bought me with Your precious blood so do what You will with my life." When we are in control, we can allow our emotions to lead us into anger, bitterness, or despair because of the things that come into our lives. But if God is in control, though we feel the pain and shed the tears, there is an indescribable peace that God will work everything out.

A grace principle is also a determining factor of what our actions will be. This principle states that those most closely involved are given the most grace, or ability, or understanding to accept the situation.

God is a God of purpose and this purpose also influences our actions. In Isaiah 55:12-13 God promises to bring good out of bad and give us such joy and peace that it should be an everlasting sign. He had a purpose to accomplish, and when we plugged into that purpose by asking Him to take over our lives, His emotions became ours to accomplish that purpose. This purpose and the accompanying grace are subject to His divine will and we are not to question Him.

The last thing is the spiritual gifts God gives you when you take Him as Saviour. One of my gifts is faith. This is an elusive word that really just means believing every word of God. Having been a student of His Word to some extent all my life, when my world seemed depopulated because one person was missing, I took His words and leaned on them. The faith He gave me was what directed me in my actions.

All of these things sway our actions concerning grief. We can show sorrow, shed tears, and mourn our loss. This is good and healthy, bringing healing. We can also become angry, bitter, and feel sorry for ourselves in our loss, and God is not pleased. But even then, if we go to God and tell Him what we feel, ask His forgiveness, accept His cleansing, and determine to seek Him. He will forgive us and wrap us in His comforting love and we will be healed.

Many times grief is multiplied because of regret. "If only I'd . . . " is the theme of our thoughts. At my brother's death, all of us realized we had become so busy with our different responsibilities that we hadn't taken the time to just say the simple words, "I love you." This added pain to our sorrow. We promised each other there beside his coffin that we would never become so busy again.

When we look back on Dana's death we see the many ways God led us to share individually in her life so we would not have this problem to deal with along with everything else.

For instance, we are Amway Distributors and we were working to build our business in the evenings after work at the station. In the fall of 1975 our business declined. If we set up an appointment to show the business to a person, he would not be home. We began to see a pattern and wondered if this was God's way of leading us out of the business. We knew He had led us to join, so we committed it to prayer. There was no definite leading, and we had more customers than we could service properly so we decided to remain unless God blocked it.

With the extra time, I attended ball games with the kids, worked with the girls on their cooking, taught Dana to crochet and needlepoint, began sewing lessons for her, played ball, and the many things you don't do when building a business. While doing these things we talked about their activities, dreamed about the future, and our growing awareness of the Lord in our lives. We discussed Biblical principles, prophecy, and any topic that entered our heads.

God knows me so well! He knew I would have felt

guilty of spending all that time helping earn money that Dana could never share in spending, rather than being with her. Now I praise Him for that lull in business for that time is worth more to me than all the gold in the world.

Renee was also glad she had taken extra time to be with Dana. On the Sunday night before Dana was killed, the Church had a musical program in which Dana was to take part. She didn't want her hair with the usual natural-curly look but wanted a smooth-body look. Normally we would not do it because it was a four-hour process and had to be sandwiched in between services. But Renee agreed and the two of them primped all afternoon. The extra care gave Dana a new confidence and she looked truly beautiful. Several people came up and remarked on how well she looked. Our pastor's wife said, "She looked just like an angel!" She was not wearing her glasses, for they were in for repair, so she kept squinting her eyes at the director to read her lips for directions. This is an endearing picture for the family but especially for Renee.

One of the most fun things we did during this time was to decide that we would make our gifts for Christmas instead of buying them. The two or three months before Christmas was a time of whispered intrigue, secrets, and stolen moments of creativity. We designated them love gifts and it was with this emotion they were made and given.

Since Dana's death, the things she made for each of us are very, very precious. For me she made a collar of strung pearls. In the very center of the front she messed up on the design and didn't notice it until she was finished. She was most embarrassed and wanted to restring it but I wouldn't let her. To me it's beautiful!

One of my most delightful memories is the ten or twenty minute snatches of time spent with my children each day. I have always felt children needed to be special to us individually as well as collectively so I developed a pattern of spending a few minutes every day with each of them. This is where I found out what was really on their hearts and minds. Even today, though they are grown, this custom continues and brings joy in my life and I hope in theirs also.

These are precious, private things. I remember one talk I had with Dana when she was about ten. She shared how happy she was that she didn't have to wonder any more whether Rod and I were going to get a divorce. I had to really contain myself to keep from betraying the surprise I felt. In questioning her it was revealed that she was aware of the current of unrest in our marriage when she was small. All she knew was that Daddy was always away (he was in pipeline construction) and when he came home all the rules changed and he was the focus of our attention. She also was aware of their noise upsetting him, and my unhappiness or anger when he would not go to church or school activities with us. Then, when he was gone again, everything went back to its regular routine. So in her mind, someday Daddy was just not coming home. She was so happy when we purchased the station and he came home for good.

Then, of course, I got myself squared away with the Lord where He could start working in our marriage. She didn't know the whys but she could feel the difference in the atmosphere. It really made me realize the far-reaching power our emotions have. I thank God she knew we had changed!

* * * * *

In the summer and early fall of 1975, I began to have thoughts come to my mind about writing a book. It was such a ridiculous idea for me that I refused to think about it. Since it kept on returning so often, I finally had to deal with it. I reasoned that since every thought comes from God or Satan, I would have to find out if this was God's will. I was too embarrassed to say anything to my family, so I waited until the Thanksgiving holidays when my sister, Nancy, was visiting, to approach the subject. I had already told the Lord that if she laughed, I was through. I told her I thought I was supposed to write a book. She didn't laugh, although later she told me how hard it had been. She then asked, "What are you going to write about?" I told her, "I don't know, that's what I wanted to talk to you about." She then proceeded to advise me to keep a diary of all the things the Lord was teaching me, allowing to happen to me, and the things I was teaching.

We had international students spend their Christmas holidays with us and we had a great time. I began a diary and included the correspondence that followed their visit.

Then early in 1976, Rod entered the race for County Judge. I began another diary about the things God was working out for us in this.

When Dana was killed, I knew this was what God had really wanted me to write about, but I didn't want to.

In June, I went to a youth camp as Assistant Recreation Leader in order to escape the public eye for a while. I was tired of talking to so many strangers at that time. I was asked to give my testimony at the camp and through this was invited to speak at a church in the area.

There was a man who stood that night during the question-and-answer period and asked me to please write a book so everyone would see the beautiful things God had done. This was my confirmation!

I began thinking about writing but every time I would sit down, I could not bring myself to put anything into words. It was the same feeling I still have about saying the actual words of what happened to Dana.

On the anniversary of her death, I tried again. I am a very factual, straight-forward person and the more emotional I feel, sometimes the more statistical I become. I wrote a newspaper report instead of a book. Everyone who read it commented on the lifelessness of it. I thought I had done all I could do so I tried to forget about it.

In May, I had to have surgery and decided to work on the manuscript again during my recuperative period, asking God to help me write the things He wanted me to write.

This time the words and tears flowed, intermingled. God took the whole incident from my subconscious to my conscious mind bringing with it the same pain, anger, and bitterness I had experienced before as well as the love, joy, and peace. There was such total recall, I could remember that one of the ladies who came had the third button from the top missing on her dress. There were times the pain seemed unbearable.

As I wrote down the feelings I was experiencing, God

brought total healing. Now I can praise God for having me write about this crisis period of my life, for as I wrote, I saw more of His plan.

This whole chain of events started with the book, so I have felt sort of in limbo, waiting for it to be published and everything considered done. Our goal as a family was to do whatever God asked of us so He would get glory. Since Dana had to die, we didn't want her suffering wasted.

I have tried to write as accurately as I could and would ask you not to make quick judgments on it or us. Some who have read it the first time through were so overcome with grief that God would allow such a thing to happen that they did not see the real meaning. The second time, they thought how great we were and felt inadequate themselves. The third time through, they saw it was not us, but God, who had done the work and knew if they had some great trial He would be sufficient for them too.

My prayer for you is that God will give you wisdom to see this magnificient truth also.

-Jean Mize

Afterword

Most of us grudgingly accept death as certain and wonder now and then what it will be like to die. Ideally, we prefer a way of dying which will allow a minimum of suffering. We prefer to die only after having lived to a ripe old age, and we covet the comforting presence of family and friends when the inevitable hour arrives.

This book is about death that was far from ideal. Dana Mize was twelve when her hour of death came suddenly and violently. Hardly an ideal way to die, we would say.

I am the Mize family's pastor, and Dana's death posed as great a challenge to my ministry as I have ever experienced. It was my place to lend comfort and reassurance to the family and friends during and after the ordeal which, under the circumstances, I felt inadequate to do. But the greatest challenge lay in answering the question that always is asked when a young person is taken away in the prime of life, and in such a merciless way: "Why did God allow this awful thing to happen?"

From the human perspective, it was impossible to reconcile the details of Dana's tragic death with the biblical revelation of a loving and all-wise God. I must admit, in fact, that the irreconcilability of a merciful God with the merciless death of a child temporarily left me in the tension of despair.

That despair drove Rod, Jean, and me to the Scriptures for answers — and if answers were not possible for the moment, then at least for comfort and reassurance. The Word of God says that "all things work together for good to them that love God" (Rom. 8:28). Could we believe that? Our faith would not allow us to believe otherwise, and we all began to surrender the entire affair into the hands of the Lord.

We soon were brought to realize that, although something very ugly had happened to Dana, something beautiful was beginning to take shape within us. That beauty first appeared in Rod and Jean on the morning after Dana's abduction. They went off to pray together, and when they returned, they remarked to me that the Lord had given them comfort and assurance out of Isaiah 55, particularly the verse which reads,

"For my thoughts are not your thoughts, neither are your ways my ways, saith the Lord."

The passage goes on to establish the immutability of God's purposes and promises as recorded in His Word.

That passage began to work a miracle in us all. It provided, initially, the strength that we needed to face the enemy of uncertainty because, for three days, we did not know what had become of Dana. Then, when her body was discovered, that same passage gave us strength and security, because the promise of eternal life is part of the immutable promise of God's Word. It also worked the miracle of peace.

The Scriptures speak of "the peace of God that passes all understanding," and how that peace sustains us even under the most trying circumstances. That peace was given to Rod and Jean, and to their children, and later to virtually our entire fellowship. It stilled the grief and rage that swept over us in waves as each new development came to light during that awful week. It calmed our hysteria and brought sweetness along with the sorrow. It was able to bring about another miracle — forgiveness — when Dana's murderer was put on trial.

This book, written by Dana's mother, carries a message of strong conviction that the promises of God are unchangeable, and that those who die in the Lord have life everlasting, regardless of the way they might have suffered physical death. That conviction has been the source of indescribable peace to Dana's family, friends, and to me. It is my prayer that this same peace will be yours as you relive our tragedy — and triumph.

Rev. W.L. Probasco,
Pastor,
First Baptist Church
Conway, Arkansas

Questions people ask . . .

I have had so many people write, call, or come to me with questions, people were sincerely seeking a fuller knowledge of God, that I chose to include a few of the ones asked most often with the answers I give.

1. How could you give Dana up so easily?

A. I had no choice about giving her up. I might have reacted differently if I had. I know God could have stopped the whole thing if it had not been in His purpose. Since I know it to be His will, if I'm submissive to that will, then I must accept her death with serenity. It has not been easy but I realize God has been preparing us for a long time. The preparation itself has been painful. God has allowed each of our children, but especially Dana, to be in circumstances where we had to stand back, helpless, and wait for Him to work out the problem. Sometimes it was in illness, sometimes it was relationships, and sometimes adverse situations. Dana and I have had many prayers together so she could go back into a problem at school or church. At times like these, I would have to say, "Lord, she's your child so you work things out for her best and protect her as you see fit."

After years of doing this, it was automatic to give her to God in this, another adverse situation where we had no control. *It was not easy, and we were not as calm inside as we appeared, but we found God sufficient!*

2. How could you have loved her and reacted the way you did to her death?

A. It is not because I loved her less that I can accept her death, but because I loved her more. True love wants only the best for the one that is loved. The best for Dana was to be totally in God's perfect will for her. That is where she was, even though in our narrow human minds, it is hard to understand, for she completed the work she was called to do. How could I desire, even for a fleeting moment, her to be here in this evil world when she is in heaven with Jesus Christ Himself? I can't, not because I love less, but because I love her so much!

3. Did you move because of the memories connected with your home?

A. No, the reason we moved was because we were driving 300-400 miles a week to Conway. We were planning to move before her death but the timing was wrong. Renee, Dana, and I were the ones to select our home. Dana and I worked hours drawing the floor plan and furniture to scale so we could decide where each piece of furniture would go. That was where they were placed when we finally moved. So her death did not bring about our move; we only carried through with something that had started prior to her death.

4. When did you decide to write a book about Dana's death?

A. I began having mental urgings about writing a book in the latter months of 1975. I ignored the thoughts, thinking them ridiculous, but they persisted. I would not tell my family for fear they would laugh. My sister was coming for the holidays and I told the Lord I was going to tell her about this strange thought. She asked what I was going to write about and I told her, "That's what I want you to help me with." She suggested I write about something I had learned, what I was doing, or something I personally knew about. I received no leading in that so she suggested I keep a diary and let God direct from that. We were working with international students and had formed some good relationships so I began my first diary. Then God led Rod to enter the local county judge race so I started another notebook. Then in April, when Dana was killed, I knew in my heart, this was what God wanted me to write. As I've claimed the mind of Christ, I've been amazed at the clarity of each incident in my mind. It has been painful, for I've had to live again the experience in order to write it, but God has used it as a means of healing. So, to be truthful, it was not my decision to write a book, neither was the subject selected by me. My decision was to do the will of God and that I have done to the best of my ability.

5. What do you think is the most important thing that helped prepare you for Dana's death?

A. I think it was knowing that death for a Christian is

really a doorway to God. Knowing this came from studying the Word, believing it came from the faith God has given us, and holding firm to it came from years of watching God's faithfulness to His word. In view of this I guess I would say the most important thing was knowing God through His word, the Bible.

6. Usually there are feelings of guilt connected with a death, not that you could have prevented it, but maybe something you would have liked to do, but didn't. Did you or members of your family experience this?

A. It is difficult to answer for my family but, yes, there were a few. Rod was out in the public all the time, being questioned about his reaction to her death until he began to wonder if he loved her like he should. During this period he wished he had spent more time with her. Bill realized it had been some time since he had told her that he loved her and this hurt for a time. Lance wished he had taken more time to do things with her. Renee had not kissed her goodnight the night before her death. I praise God they were such small regrets. So far, perhaps because of my involvement in the lives of my family, I have had none of these. If something does surface later, I pray I can take it to God and let Him give me peace again.

7. Why do you think God tests us?

A. Until a few years ago, I thought it was for Him to determine our growth record, but through studying about Abraham in Genesis, I discovered the fallacy of this. God knew beforehand how Abraham would react but Abraham did not. The obvious conclusion is for us to know where we are on our growth scale. This will reveal areas where we need more work. So, one reason is for our being perfected. Another is so that when God solves our problem He will receive glory for it. A third is when we go through our testing triumphantly, Christ in us will be revealed to a world in need of Christ. In all three ways, as others see Christ alive and working in us, they will desire His work in their lives also.

8. You always seem so happy. Do you think about Dana? Don't you have times when you really miss her?

A. I am happy, I do think about her, and I do miss her but not the way I expected to. I know Dana is as alive as my other children. Renee and Bill are away at work, Lance is away at school, and Dana is away in heaven. As surely as I will see my other children again, I will see her also. My wait will only be longer. Her absence has taught me a very valuable lesson of God's care. Now when I'm away from home I can more confidently leave my family in His care. As surely as He cares for Dana, He cares for the rest of my family. Then someday we will all be reunited and with Him.

9. How can I tell my children about death so they can understand?

A. First you must have a full understanding yourself so you radiate confidence and not fear when you talk to them. Also, remember I am talking about a Christian's death. The Christian does not actually *experience* death for Christ has already conquered it; therefore, we just cease our existence here and begin it in another place. It is said that one split second after death we are more alive, more aware than we've ever been in our lifetime. Death is a release into life infinitely greater than anything we've ever known.

This is the way I explained it to my children when they were small:

"When you were little do you remember going to sleep on the floor or sofa but when you woke up that was not where you were? While you slept someone lovingly gathered you in his arms and put you to bed. That is the same way death is. Just as you closed your eyes in sleep, death will come to each one of us some day, and when we 'wake up' we will be in our new home, called Heaven. When you open your eyes, you will see Jesus and the angels."

God bless you!